CHAIRS THAT STAND EMPTY

CHAIRS THAT STAND EMPTY

THE MEN BEHIND THE NAMES ON THE HULME HALL FIRST WORLD WAR MEMORIAL

JAMES HERN

Copyright © 2017 James Hern

The moral right of the author has been asserted.

Apart from any fair dealing for the purposes of research or private study, or criticism or review, as permitted under the Copyright, Designs and Patents Act 1988, this publication may only be reproduced, stored or transmitted, in any form or by any means, with the prior permission in writing of the publishers, or in the case of reprographic reproduction in accordance with the terms of licences issued by the Copyright Licensing Agency. Enquiries concerning reproduction outside those terms should be sent to the publishers.

Matador
9 Priory Business Park,
Wistow Road, Kibworth Beauchamp,
Leicestershire. LE8 0RX
Tel: 0116 279 2299
Email: books@troubador.co.uk
Web: www.troubador.co.uk/matador
Twitter: @matadorbooks

ISBN 978 1785898 433

British Library Cataloguing in Publication Data.
A catalogue record for this book is available from the British Library.

Printed and bound by CPI Group (UK) Ltd, Croydon, CR0 4YY
Typeset in 11pt Gill Sans by Troubador Publishing Ltd, Leicester, UK

Matador is an imprint of Troubador Publishing Ltd

This book is dedicated to the memory of Hulme Hall Wardens Rev John Henry Hopkinson (Warden from 1903 to 1914) and Rev Thomas Nicklin (1914 to 1937) who witnessed the suffering that the First World War brought to the Hulme Hall community.

Without their meticulous record-keeping it would not have been possible to capture so much detail about the lives of those who fought.

Some day the war will be over and we shall meet again – or we shall meet if we can bear to face the chairs that will stand empty. For, although to serve England in war is a glorious thing, war in itself is only ugly and pitiless and hateful. There are some who will not come back from the war. The death of those who have fallen is the supreme and incorruptible treasure of the Hall for all the future, but for the present it is only pain. We know that they died gladly, and we must greet them gladly in their new life across the gulf of death.

*Bid them forward, breast and back as either should be. "Strive and thrive!" cry
"Speed, - fight on, fare ever
    There as here!"*

Rev J H Hopkinson – January 1916
Hulme Hall Warden 1903–1914

FOREWORD

Captain David Wiseman
The Yorkshire Regiment

Hulme Hall 2001–2002
Manchester University 2001–2005

David Wiseman studied at The University of Manchester between 2001 and 2005 and spent his first year housed at Hulme Hall, completing his studies with a Bachelor of Arts Degree with Honours in Economic and Social Studies.

Whilst at Hulme Hall, David joined the Manchester and Salford University Officer Training Corps, igniting a passion that resulted in him joining the army straight from university. David commissioned into The Yorkshire Regiment in 2006 and commanded light infantrymen in both Iraq and Afghanistan. During a heavy fire fight with the Taliban in Helmand Province 2009, Captain Wiseman was shot in the chest suffering life-threatening injuries.

David's injuries proved to be career ending and after several operations and months of intense rehabilitation he was medically discharged from the British Army. However, he was inspired by fellow members of the wounded community who flat-out refused to be beaten by their injuries and who used sport and adventurous challenge to regain their identities. David took up this challenge and began climbing in the Alps before successfully summiting the eighth highest mountain in the world, Mount Manaslu (8163m), and attempting Mount Everest (8850m).

David now works for the Royal Foundation of The Duke and Duchess of Cambridge and Prince Harry. One of his tasks is to manage the Endeavour Fund, through which he hopes many other wounded service personnel and veterans will be inspired to use sport and adventure as a vehicle for recovery. David was a key member of the Invictus Games organising committee and also won four medals during the inaugural international sporting competition.

You can read more about David Wiseman's story in the book Helmand to the Himalayas *published by Osprey Publishing.*

As a boy learning about the Great War, I found it hard to understand what drove men to leave everything behind to join the ever-hungry war machine that demanded more and more soldiers in Europe. The hardest thing I found to grasp was the idea that for these men it was all a fantastic adventure with glory to be found just around the corner. Yet time and time again that illusion came crashing down in the realisation of what was waiting for them across the Channel. Could they not anticipate what hell they were launching themselves into?

Like all young men, it was a lesson I failed to learn for myself because as a soldier reflecting back on the Great War, I could fully understand what impulse grabbed these men and pushed them to sign up. It was the same hunger that I experienced looking forward to combat with the certainty that the risks and perils would be overshadowed by the excitement and thrill of engaging the enemy at close quarters.

My limited experience in the face of the enemy is dwarfed in comparison to the months and years of threat that the men of the Great War endured. Although I feel a sense of connection with these men who also fought and bled for their country, I am truly honoured to have been asked to contribute to a book that represents those who gave everything for a nation that still remembers their actions and mourns their loss today.

Chairs That Stand Empty is a book that allows the reader to look to the past and remember. It is right that we look to the past and it is right that we remember. To do anything else would be dishonourable, disrespectful and dangerous – as failing to remember is failing to learn from previous conflicts.

As a member of the Hulme Hall alumni, I feel a greater connection to the men in the book, helping us to remember them as people rather than numbers on a table, or long forgotten names carved into stone.

I sincerely hope that in a hundred years, someone will look back at the wars in which I have fought and write something akin to *Chairs That Stand Empty* about the friends I have lost over the past decade. Through compiling such an account, James has demonstrated the deepest respect for those who have paid the ultimate sacrifice in service for their country.

ONE HUNDRED YEARS ON

Continuing to Remember

> He held on to his trench until the enemy were actually in it, right to left. Most of his men having been killed or buried under the ruins of the parapet, I consider his conduct on this occasion most praiseworthy.
> Statement of commendation regarding Second Lieutenant James Henderson MC; Hulme Hall 1912–1914; following action near Ypres, 8 May 1915.[1]

With the centenary of the First World War upon us, it remains important, now more than ever, that both current and alumni members of Hulme Hall pause to remember and celebrate the lives of fellow students who were unable to fulfil the dreams and ambitions that brought them to Hulme Hall.

As the years since peace broke out have passed, so too have the memories of those who fought and died faded. The Hulme Hall War Memorial, currently residing in the Chapel, is the only reminder of those linked to the Hall who failed to return to study or continue in their chosen career. Names that once stirred memories of friendship and academic or sporting success have become simply unknown names on a memorial that residents may not even know exists.

The trail of letters, telegrams and photographs left behind by our predecessors and their families speak of the pain and heartbreak experienced throughout the war years and remind us that the stories of these men's lives should not yet be consigned to the pages of history.

But without the personal stories of those who served and died, we cannot begin to remember or appreciate the sacrifices that were made.

Best friends Wilfred Trevelyan and James Henderson left Hulme Hall upon receiving commissions with the Rifle Brigade in August 1914. They witnessed the destruction of Ypres, in Belgium, during the Second Battle of Ypres in

April 1915 and would have heard first hand the horror stories and rumours circulating of a new weapon employed by the enemy, as gas was used for the first time on the Western Front. Trevelyan was killed shortly afterwards, in early May, whilst Henderson went on to distinguish himself in holding off waves of German attacks alongside the Canadian Army only days after the death of his friend.

Henderson served for a further sixteen months, being wounded on two separate occasions and mentioned in dispatches for his work. He was killed in action on 18 August 1916 during the Battle of the Somme shortly after capturing an enemy machine gun single-handed. On that same day, nineteen-year-old Private Robert Southward was killed only a few miles away from Henderson, a victim of friendly fire when his Battalion moved across no man's land to attack an enemy trench near High Wood. Robert had only been in France for sixteen days after leaving Hulme Hall in March that year to begin training.

Robert Bedford wrote a series of letters to Professor Tout, his History tutor at Victoria University of Manchester, between 1915 and 1918, telling of the horrors of witnessing his friends' bodies lying in no man's land after a failed attack in Gallipoli, the extreme boredom with army life when not in action, his guilt in not fighting in France whilst stationed in the Sinai Desert and the sensations of witnessing the devastated countryside and villages following the German withdrawal to the Hindenburg Line in early 1917.

It took Howard Harker several years to have his application accepted to join the Royal Flying Corps, his work with the experimental department of the Royal Aircraft Factory being considered a reserved occupation. He later fought against Baron von Richthofen's 'flying circus' squadron during the Battle of Arras in 1917, losing a close friend to Von Richthofen himself a few months later. An accomplished pilot, Howard survived the war only to succumb to the influenza epidemic that claimed more lives between 1918 and 1919 than four years of conflict.

At home, the families of those serving overseas continued in their day-to-day lives, fearing the arrival of a telegram from the War Office; news that would be likely to bring their nightmares and worst fears to reality, that their son, brother or husband had been wounded, killed, or reported as missing in action. The Henderson family would have become accustomed to hearing from the War Office, receiving over a dozen telegrams reporting of James being wounded or admitted to hospital, before finally receiving the news of his death in August 1916.

George Hebblethwaite was reported missing on 7 July 1916. His family were only notified a week after this date and had to wait a further agonising six weeks before receiving news that, following an investigation, George had officially been classified as being killed in action.

Having been married to Harold in Australia shortly after his enlistment and before he headed to England, Muriel Swift only learned of her husband's death after seeing his name in a list of casualties published in the local paper a month after it occurred.

Although the story of each of the men in this book is ultimately a sad one, there are moments that remind us of the human side of those who went to war.

Harold Swift was found guilty of going absent without leave for nine days on his arrival in England from Australia. When in France, he was fined a day's pay for urinating in a public place. Murray Chapman was branded unsuitable officer material by his superiors, and was involved in a number of aircraft accidents. Godfrey Hemsley was court marshalled for being drunk on duty and Arthur Lord served overseas underage, lying about his age on a number of occasions afterwards.

When you next pause to observe a minute silence during Remembrance Day, spare a thought and remember the boys of Hulme Hall who never returned.

ACKNOWLEDGEMENTS

"He was a very capable officer, knew his work well and was very brave. I had the utmost confidence in him. He told me that he wished to be where there was fighting to be done."

Major J H Edwards, writing about Second Lieutenant Godfrey Hamilton Hemsley, Hulme Hall 1905–1908, after his death in October 1917.[2]

Although I didn't know it at the time, the decision on a freezing autumn evening on the Somme in 2010 to research the names on the Hulme Hall War Memorial would have a tremendous impact on my life.

My interest in Hulme Hall's involvement in the First World War began whilst I served as Chapel Steward for two years when living at the Hall between 2001 and 2004. One of the responsibilities of the role involved organising the annual Hulme Hall Remembrance Day service, and included reading out the names of those on the war memorial who died during both the First and Second World Wars.

Gareth Williams, my predecessor as Chapel Steward, had previously undertaken research into the men on the War Memorial, publishing information in the Remembrance Day service sheet. Whilst the names of the places where men were killed sounded familiar, such as the Somme, Ypres and Gallipoli, I remember a feeling of dissatisfaction at the unanswered questions raised by the tantalising glimpses into their stories. Particularly vivid were the names of James Henderson, Arthur Lord and Allan Higson Smith.

> **Captain Arthur Lord, 3rd Bn, Welsh Regiment.**
> Entered Hall in October 1914, reading medicine
> Wounded at Ypres, October 1915; wounded on the Somme, July 1916.
> Died of wounds at Poperinghe, Belgium: 12 February 1917. Age 19.

Arthur Lord was only nineteen when he died in February 1917, yet he was wounded at Ypres in 1915 and had been promoted to the rank of Captain by the time he died. Surely the age shown on the service sheet was an error, or was he really underage when he first arrived in France?

> **Second Lieutenant James Grieg Mitchell Henderson, 4th Bn, Rifle Brigade.**
> Entered Hall in October 1912, studying chemistry
> Wounded at Ypres, August 1915; awarded Military Cross.
> Killed in action at Delville Wood, Somme, France: 18 August 1916. Age 22.

What was James Henderson's story? Why was he awarded the Military Cross? How was he wounded at Ypres?

> **Captain Allan Higson Smith, 21st Sqn, Royal Flying Corps.**
> Entered Hall in October 1912, studying engineering
> Wounded on the Somme, July 1916; awarded the Military Cross.
> Killed in action near Lens, Pas-de-Calais, France: 21 August 1917. Age 23.

Allan Smith was wounded on the Somme and also served in the Royal Flying Corps. Did he fight during the first day of the Somme offensive on 1 July 1916? Was he flying at the time or had he transferred to the RFC from the infantry afterwards?

It wasn't until 2010 that the embers of these unanswered questions were ignited during a day trip to France which involved a brief, and unplanned, visit to the Somme. Viewing the gentle undulating countryside, I realised that I didn't understand what had happened here; either in July 1916, during the first day of the infamous Battle of the Somme, or the subsequent battles through to the end of 1918. What made this unremarkable landscape worth sacrificing the lives of thousands of young men?

Wanting to find out more about the Somme, and the First World War in general, I saw researching the lives of the names I had read out at the Remembrance Day services as a way to do this. Little did I realise that over six years after starting a project to satisfy personal curiosities, I would be in a position to publish the stories of those men in an effort to ensure their lives and stories are not forgotten.

As well as studying documents and letters at both the University of Manchester Library and the National Archives in Kew, my research has taken me from various cemeteries across England, Wales, France and Belgium to visit the graves and memorials of the Hulme Hall men. I have met some fascinating people during my journeys and have also had the privilege of corresponding with relatives of a number of the fallen men.

Over time, I realised that with the level of information I was uncovering, along with the unfolding stories of courage, strength and heartbreak, I had a responsibility to share them.

Having spoken at the 105th Annual Hulme Hall Alumni Dinner in 2014, I see publishing this book as a way in which the men's lives can continue to inspire a wider audience of Hulme Hall alumni, current residents and those who will enter the Hall in the future, to discover that they are part of the rich history of an institution that has existed for over 145 years.

The information in this book far from paints the full picture of everything that happened to the Hulme Hall community throughout the war. Detailed research is yet to be carried out on the lives of those from Hulme Hall who fought and survived. The Hulme Hall Chronicles covering this period offer a fascinating glimpse into the stories of those who fought and survived, with many awarded the Military Cross, being wounded in action, being affected by gas or suffering from shell shock. A short summary of only a very few of these stories is captured later in this book. Perhaps this may spark an interest in someone else to uncover the stories of those who survived, and how the war subsequently impacted on their lives.

That I have been able to uncover what I have, and put these findings into print, is down to the support of wide array of people without whom this book would not have been possible.

Hulme Hall / The University of Manchester

Without the research undertaken by Gareth Williams in the late 1990s and early 2000s, it is unlikely this project would ever have taken place. Gareth's research and presentation of details in the Hulme Hall remembrance service sheets were the prompt that in 2001 set in motion the events that have led to this publication.

Hulme Hall Wardens Jackie Wilson and Mike Mercer, who gave me their support and blessing to undertake research on behalf of the Hulme Hall community.

James Hopkins, University Historian and Heritage Manager, for his ongoing support and encouragement.

Pen Richardson, who has commenced a tremendous undertaking in researching the names of all the fallen on the Manchester University war memorials. The stories of all those from the Victoria Manchester University and UMIST will be captured on the dedicated University of Manchester World War 1 website: www.ww1.manchester.ac.uk.

The University of Manchester Library who have provided permission to publish textual and photographic materials held in the library archives.

Other members of the Hulme Hall or University of Manchester community whom I owe a great deal include: Robert Quale, David Wiseman, Phil Atkinson and committee members of both the Hulme Hall Alumni Association and Hulme Hall Trust.

Families of the Fallen

Making contact with the families of some of the Hulme Hall men who were killed has been a great privilege, and I have been grateful for the information, support and encouragement they have provided.

I'm particularly indebted to the following family members: John Cunliffe and Sandy Nicholson (Earnest Cunliffe). Hazel Newton (Arthur Davies), Alan Wildblood, Stephen Charles Wildblood, Cedric Wildblood (William Wildblood), Jeremy Coke-Smyth (Eyre Wilkinson), Graham Holton and Ruth Holton (Alfred Holton), Deb Walker (George Hebblethwaite), Michael Watts and Catherine Johnson (Harland Watts), Ronald Barry (Kenneth Barry) and Donna Merrill (Robert Southall).

Others

Renfrey Pearson (Ernest Cunliffe), John W Hawkins (Arthur Davies) Jim Massey and The Staffordshire Regiment Museum (Arthur Davies), Celia Wolfe and Akworth School (Harold Swift), National Archives of Australia (Harold Swift), Peter Harrold and Lincoln Christ's Hospital School (Godfrey Hemsley), Phil Wood and Newbury History, The British Newspaper Archive (William Freemantle), Susan Pares, Mike Senior (Harry Pickles), Laureen

Wreggitt (Harry Pickles) Levantine Heritage website (Alfred Holton), Upper Hopton Parish (George Hebblethwaite), Gillian White (Harland Watts), Jane and ww1photos.com (Allan Higson Smith and Thomas Fawsitt), Chris Reynolds (Arthur Lord), Ed Stephenson (James Blue), Justine Taylor, Archivist at the Honourable Artillery Company headquarters, London (James Blue), Marlborough College Archives (Arthur Marshall), Andrew Dawrant and the Royal Aero Club Trust (Howard Harker and Murray Chapman), Amanda Taylor (William Warrington), Berenice Baynham, warmemorials.myfastforum.org (Noel Gornell), Janet Hoskyns (Gilbert Budden) Ashley Hern, for writing the section entitled 'The Great War: 1914–1919' and Chris Barltrop.

I have accessed a wide range of materials during my research; the majority, if not all, are recorded in the bibliography, sources and end notes.

Whilst I have made an effort to record all source information and request and receive permission from appropriate copyright holders, there may be incidents where I have not contacted the correct or appropriate person. If this is the case, I would be pleased to correct any errors or omissions in future editions.

— — —

I particularly want to acknowledge and thank Linda for her ongoing support and encouragement throughout this project. Linda was with me on that cold autumn evening in 2010 and has been a great source of support and encouragement since, showing enthusiasm and interest as I have dragged her across the battlefields of Belgium and France and numerous graveyards scattered across the UK.

Even after the birth of our beautiful daughter Annabelle, Linda has ensured I've had time and space to finish this project. For this, I'll be forever grateful.

HISTORY OF HULME HALL

1691 to present day

> Hulme Hall is established under the Scheme of the Charity Commissioners for regulating the Hulme Trust Estates, and has a substantial endowment there from. Its object is to provide for University students board, residence, and tutorial supervision, and also those advantages of corporate life and companionship which are associated with the College life of the older Universities.
>
> *Extract from 1908 Hulme Hall Prospective* [3]

This summary of the history of Hulme Hall has been composed from numerous sources and articles, including the 1908 and 1920 Hulme Hall prospectives and an article entitled 'Pioneer Hall of Residence in Manchester' written by Dr G N Burkhardt in February 1970. [4]

Founding of The University of Manchester

Owens College was founded in 1851, and in 1880 joined the newly established federal Victoria University for the North of England. University College Liverpool joined in 1884 and Yorkshire College, Leeds followed in 1887.

In 1903, University College Liverpool left Victoria University to create the University of Liverpool, with Yorkshire College, Leeds following suit a year later, founding the University of Leeds. With only Owens College now linked to the University for the North of England, the two were merged to become the Victoria University of Manchester.

In 2004, the Victoria University of Manchester merged with the University of Manchester Institute of Science and Technology (UMIST), becoming the present day University of Manchester.

Founding of Hulme Hall

The roots of Hulme Hall were laid in 1691 with the death of William Hulme, a prominent landowner and lawyer from the Greater Manchester area. His only son having died at the age of fifteen, William left his property to his trustees and their heirs; the money was to be used for educational purposes. The Hulme Charitable Trust started by providing Hulmeian scholarships at Brasenose College, Oxford, with a decision to limit awards to the sons of Lancashire clergy.

From 1869, William Houldsworth, an Owens College Trustee, and Hugh Birley, a Member of Parliament for Manchester, were the driving force behind the establishment of a Church of England Hall of Residence for students of Owens College.

In December 1869, Houldsworth and Birley, with Joseph Greenwood, the Principal of Owens College, and Oliver Heywood, the Treasurer of the Owens Extension Appeal and later of the College, met Hulme Trustees to discuss support for the proposed Hall. The Hulme Trustees, although sympathised with the plan, stated with regret that under the powers they then had they were precluded from helping, but also that they expected in the near future to promote a fresh Act of Parliament which would authorise such assistance.

It was decided to go ahead with the Hall regardless. The provisional committee, set up in January 1870, had Birley as Chairman, Heywood as Treasurer, Houldsworth and Professor Richard Christie as Secretaries, and included the Principal and altogether seven of the eleven Trustees of Owens College. The Bishop, Dean and Archdeacon of Manchester accepted invitations to join them later in that year. They, and subsequently some sixteen individuals, nearly all from this group, subscribed personally £4,700 towards the enterprise.

By 1875, the committee found themselves with a hall some £600 in debt and with no sign of resources other than their own pockets. The Hall was closed. After further negotiations, the buildings and furniture were assigned to Houldsworth personally with the hope that he would hold them for the great day when the Hall would be reopened. In the outcome he did just this, for twelve years.

In 1881, the Charity Commission, the government department responsible for regulating registered charities, empowered the Hulme Trust to establish three schools in the Manchester area – William Hulme's Grammar

School, Hulme Grammar School and Bury Grammar School – and, as had been agreed in principle in 1869, a Hall of Residence for Anglican students at Owens College, to be known as Hulme Hall. The Hall received from the Hulme Trust £1000 per year, at least half to be devoted to scholarships.

Hulme Hall was first opened in January 1887, on the site in Plymouth Grove that had been assigned to Houldsworth. The first Warden was the Rev E L Hicks, who later became Canon of Manchester. Hicks resigned as Warden in 1892 and was succeeded by Dr E B England who held the Wardenship until 1903.

In 1906, with the demand for rooms having outgrown the accommodation available on the old site, the Hall Governors decided to erect a new building to hold sixty students. A larger site was selected in Oxford Place, Victoria Park, a residential area somewhat less than a mile from the newly formed Victoria University of Manchester and directly connected with it by tramcar. Plans were prepared for a building thoroughly collegiate in character and specially designed for a Hall of Residence. Of this building, known as Houldsworth, the greater part containing rooms for forty students and three tutors was opened in July 1907.

Three subsequent stages are notable in the development of Hulme Hall. The first came after 1918 when two large houses adjacent to the Hall, Oxford Lodge and Park House, were acquired to raise the number of students to 150 to meet the post-war rush to the university. Around a decade later, the neighbouring property, Oaklands, was added to the Hall after the closure of the Fielding Demonstration School.

The seven-acre island site so obtained was the essential asset for the second main expansion. In the 1950s it became clear that halls such as Hulme Hall could not expect to attract capital for improvement to current standards. The three old houses which formed a substantial part of the room accommodation at Hulme Hall were nearing the end of their tolerable life. So, in 1962, Hulme Hall was transferred to the university. By 1967, the university had completed building and development work to provide accommodation for 350 students through the addition of five new blocks; three named after founders of Hulme Hall – Burley, Greenwood, and Christie – with Plymouth block marking the location of the first hall in Plymouth Grove and Oaklands named after the building demolished to make room for the new accommodation. Despite being a secular institution, the university acknowledged the Christian foundations on which the Hall was founded with the construction of a new chapel.

With the decision to admit females to Hulme Hall in the 1980s, a third expansion was undertaken to increase capacity further with the construction of Burkhardt House, and provision of a theatre and conference centre, known as the John Hartshorne Centre, which were opened in February 1993.

To this day, Hulme Hall continues to be a thriving hub for students from across the UK and the world.

The pioneers would have reason to be gratified.

CALM BEFORE THE STORM

1913–14 Academic Year

> I should very much like to have another 'shot' at my thesis. Unfortunately, however, I have to take final LLB [Bachelor of Laws degree] in June 1913. After the final I shall have plenty of time to spare, but I should not be able to do much before. I will endeavour to come and see you early next week to talk the matter over.
>
> *Harry Pickles; Hulme Hall 1907–1910; in a letter to History tutor Professor Thomas Tout in October 1912* [5]

The start of the 1913–1914 academic year at Hulme Hall was as normal as any other had been throughout the previous twenty-five years since the Hall reopened in 1887.

Fifty undergraduates, seven graduates (including two university lecturers from South Africa undertaking research for the renowned Professor Rutherford) and two tutors were resident for the year, governed by the Rev J H Hopkinson who began his final year as Warden, having already completed a decade in the role.

Academically the year was a success, with three students graduating as Masters of Arts, four as Bachelors of Arts, eight as Bachelors of Science and one as a Bachelor of Commerce. Robert Montagnan, a French student who had been studying Paper Manufacture in the School of Technology, obtained a Certificate of Technology.

The Senior Man for the year, Francis John Stafford, received a First Class pass in the examination for the Teacher's Diploma and was appointed as German Master at the Manchester Municipal Secondary School (now the Manchester High School for Girls) on Wilmslow Road. He was also appointed as a resident tutor at Hulme Hall for the following academic year. Evan Clifford Williams passed his teaching degree and was appointed as Science Master at

Clifton College in Bristol. Williams' appointment was a source of pride for the Hulme Hall community as;

> One of the great public schools, which have hitherto been reluctant to admit Manchester students to their teaching staff, should appoint a student direct from Hulme Hall.
> Hulme Hall Warden's report for 1913–14 by Rev J H Hopkinson [6]

Elsewhere, former Senior Man Harold Pickles' career continued to flourish. Awarded Honours in the Solicitors' Final Examination of the Law Society, he was awarded the Clement's Inn and Daniel Reardon prizes and was appointed as Lecturer at Victoria University of Manchester for special courses on portions of Stephen's Commentaries.

The Warden continued to keep track of the career progression of other Hall alumni. Edward Quine was appointed as Headmaster of the Fieldens Demonstration School, a training school for the Department of Education of the Victoria University of Manchester, located next to Hulme Hall. Former post-graduate student Dr Niels Bohr, who had lived in Hulme Hall whilst undertaking research with Professor Rutherford, was appointed as Reader of Mathematical Physics at the university. (Dr Bohr would go on to be awarded the Nobel Prize for Physics in 1922.)

William Freemantle continued work as an Assistant Analytical Chemist at Davyhulme Sewage Treatment Works in Trafford, Greater Manchester, where he worked under Dr Gilbert J Fowler, an internationally renowned expert in sewage and bacteriology.

Not all news reported that year was positive: John Townley Millers, resident at Hulme Hall between 1907 and 1910 when studying Chemistry, died whilst working with the Indian Forest Service in Muree, India.

At least four members of the Hall – Stephen Fisher, Aurbrey Harris, Evan Williams and William Trevelyan – were regulars in the 1st XV University Rugby team, whilst James Henderson turned out regularly for the 2nd XV. The 1st XV were victorious in the Christie Shield competition against rival universities Liverpool and Leeds.

In a review of the 1913–1914 rugby season published in the Manchester University Magazine, the author described Trevelyan as:

> 'A quick and active dribbler with some cleverness in kicking and passing. Has come on since last season and has played consistently well during the season. Useful in the lineout. Performed the duties of junior secretary with distinction.'

No mention is made in the Hall records of any sporting successes against arch rivals Dalton Hall, against whom annual fixtures in football, rugby, athletics, tennis and swimming were played. The Hall did have a hard tennis court laid within the grounds during the session which was hoped would help maintain fitness levels throughout the winter months.

Other students enjoyed spending free time exploring other interests, with a number becoming members of the University Historical Society, led by Professor Tout. Meetings were held regularly and the group would often meet socially at the Freeman Public House. In early 1914 Hulme Hall's Robert Bedford gave a presentation on 'Trade with Spain during the reign of Elizabeth' during one of their meetings.

— — —

Away from academic and sporting pursuits, twenty-six students from the Hall were members of the Manchester University Officer Training Corps (OTC). One of the highlights of the year was the two-week summer camp, held with other OTC units from across Britain.

In July 1914, the summer camp took place at Windmill Hill on Salisbury Plain. Hulme Hall students and other members of the Manchester University OTC were joined by over 1200 cadets from eight universities and colleges, including London, Birmingham, Bristol, Leeds, Nottingham and Sheffield.

With Europe hovering on the brink of war following the assassination of Archduke Franz Ferdinand in Sarajevo in June, the uncertainty of whether Britain would be drawn into the conflict caused considerable excitement and apprehension to those cadets attending the camp, as described afterwards in the *Manchester University Magazine*:

> The battalion was certain of good training under the command of the late Major Christie and with Captain Forster, our new adjutant, as Camp Adjutant gave promise of being a most successful one, although the crisis, which Europe was passing, disturbed the work considerably.

On 2 August, the Belgian government received an ultimatum from Germany to allow free passage of their troops to France, or face occupation. Ready to defend Belgium, Britain began to mobilise, declaring war two days later when Germany invaded. With the news of impending hostility, plans for the remainder of the summer camp were cancelled as the country mobilised for war. The article in the Manchester University Magazine continued:

> On Monday the 3rd August 1914 orders were received to break up camp and in a few hours the Manchester Contingent had entrained and reached Manchester on the Monday evening. The second week of camp was therefore abandoned and the regular army officers attached to contingents were recalled to their regiments for mobilisation and subsequent embarkation to France for service with the British Expeditionary Force.

Having arrived back in Manchester, The OTC headquarters were opened in order to process 95% of students who had volunteered at camp to serve in the war [7]. Despite their keenness, the War Office could not handle the number of applicants for commissions in the initial rush of recruits. Whilst some members of Hulme Hall were accepted, others had to find different ways to join the Armed Forces to ensure they could serve in a war 'certain to be won by Christmas'.

William Freemantle, resident at Hulme Hall between 1907 and 1910, was on holiday visiting his parents in Newbury when war with Germany was declared. An officer with the 7th Battalion Manchester Regiment, he was recalled to the Territorial unit who were swiftly posted to Egypt to free up regular Army Battalions for service in France and Belgium. Speaking to a reporter of the Manchester Evening News upon mobilisation, Freemantle said:

> Anyone else can be sorry about this war, but if I have to leave the army after it is over, I don't care how long it lasts.[8]

Ten months later, William was killed in action in Gallipoli.

NOTHING BUT HONOUR

Hulme Hall and the First World War

> Rev J H Hopkinson, with the sanction of the Bishop of Manchester, joined the East Lancashire Regiment, as a private, in June 1918. He was transferred later to the Royal Army Medical Corps.
> *Miscellaneous note in the 1916–1920 Hulme Hall Chronicle about the former Hulme Hall Warden* [9]

It has been estimated that over 250 residents and staff of Hulme Hall served in the Allied Forces between 1914 and 1919. The estimate accounts for over 40% of the total number of students passing through the Hall since it was reopened in 1887 and 1919.

Moritz Pfeffer is the only known German national to attend Hulme Hall pre-1914 [10]. Entering halls in 1900, Moritz left in 1901 to join the German Navy; however, it is not known whether he was still serving in 1914.

Forty of those who served are known to have died during the conflict, either as a direct result of enemy action or an illness contracted during service.

The first killed was Second Lieutenant Wilfred Trevelyan, who was hit by shrapnel whilst organising the repair of a communication trench near Ypres in May 1915. The last to die was Major Ernest Cunliffe in March 1919, who passed away in the Lake District after contracting an illness having served in hospitals in both Manchester and on the Western Front.

Francis Stafford, Senior Student in 1913, writing in January 1916, captured the mood of pride and sorrow of those fighting and dying at Hulme Hall in the foreword for the 1914–1915 Hulme Hall Chronicle: [11]

> The Chronicle is issued this year from a Hall much depleted in numbers, but prouder than ever of the men who have gone from it. Though the war has taken its toll of our best, whose loss we regret deeply, it has brought out

the best that was in them and in all Hall men who are out fighting, and the record has brought us nothing but honour.

Seeing that the Chronicle is only published annually, it is perhaps not too early to mention in this number that there is a proposal to erect a permanent memorial in the Hall to those of our men who have fallen in the war. The proposal has not taken any definite shape as yet, and expression of opinion on the matter will be welcomed.

The three Hulme Hall Chronicles that cover the period of the war, along with the Manchester University Roll of Service that was published in 1922, provide a snapshot into the lives of many of those from Hulme Hall who fought.

At least seventeen men were awarded the Military Cross, two the Military Medal with thirteen being mentioned in dispatches. Major Francis Philip Slater and Captain William Hughes Perkins were both mentioned in dispatches on two separate occasions.

Eight foreign awards were bestowed upon Hulme Hall men, including the Légion d'honneur and Croix de Guerre. Frank Winston lived in Russia before 1914. Serving in Royal Navy Intelligence, he served along the Russian forces, being bestowed their 3rd Class Order of St Anne award in 1915 and 2nd Class order of St Stanislaus in 1916.

Whilst approximately 10% of Hulme Hall men who served did so with the Royal Army Medical Corps,[12] a number went on to use their knowledge of chemistry to serve with the Royal Engineers gas warfare units.

Second Lieutenant James Edgar Kemp was shot down whilst serving with the Royal Air Force in September 1918 and taken prisoner. He was repatriated in December that year. Royal Engineer Sapper John Hay Helm was also captured and saw out the conflict in a prisoner-of-war camp.

Many Hulme Hall men were wounded. Lieutenant Albert James Ralph served with the 10th Battalion South Wales Borderers. He was wounded, before later being invalided home through shell shock, as was Alfred Kenneth Hughes, who served as a Second Lieutenant with the East York Regiment.

Yves Marie Bozellec was seriously wounded in the leg in September 1915, having returned to his native France to fight with the Régiment d'Infanterie Coloniale. He was hospitalised for eight months before being discharged, joining his old firm, the Calico Printers' Association in Manchester.

Rowland Charles Fielding and Victor Edward Hugh Lindesay both arrived in Manchester in 1888, becoming the twenty-eighth and twenty-ninth residents of the newly refurbished Hulme Hall respectively. During the war, both were to serve as Lieutenant-Colonels.

Fielding, when leaving for France in 1915, began writing what would become hundreds of letters to his wife describing his experiences in the trenches, and those of his men, in great detail. In 2001, Jonathan Walker compiled and edited Fielding's letters, publishing them in a book entitled *War Letters to a Wife*.[13]

Many other Hulme Hall men left a written trail of their experiences. Several History students wrote to their tutor, Professor Tout, including Francis Swinnerton Cook who served mainly in Mesopotamia after training with the Royal Army Medical Corps. Robert Bedford wrote of his time serving alongside Harry Thomas Cawley, who was the Member of Parliament for Heywood, Lancashire. Cawley was killed in Gallipoli, with Robert being one of the first on the scene.

Charles George Awdry Cory wrote diaries throughout his life, which cover his time with the Royal Flying Corps and Royal Air Force. These diaries are held at the Nelson Mandela Metropolitan University in South Africa.

Ronald James Cornish, Senior Man during the Christmas Term in 1921, served with the Royal Garrison Artillery. He later served as Head of Department of Municipal Engineering at the Manchester Municipal College of Technology (later UMIST).

Harry Cotton served in the Meteorological Section of the Royal Engineers. In the book entitled *Behind the Front: British Soldiers and French Civilians, 1914–1918*, by Craig Gibson, the author notes [14]:

> A Meteorological officer attached to General Headquarters ('Meteor'), Corporal Harry Cotton wrote poignantly in the 1970s about his wartime romance. He describes his posting to a village, becoming friends with a local family, falling in love with the daughter, including a description of the consummation of their relationship and finally being posted elsewhere, where he received news of the woman's death: 'Thinking about it later I realised that it was a good thing, providential perhaps as far as I was concerned, for I realised that I had certainly allowed myself to become far too emotionally attached'.

Perhaps one of the most captivating stories of the Hulme Hall men belongs to Gilbert Budden. Employed as a mining engineer in Mexico in August 1914, he returned to Britain and was commissioned into the Royal Engineers in April 1915. Three months later he had been posted to France. The following year he transferred to the Royal Flying Corps, qualifying as a pilot in early 1917. Only a month later, he was hospitalised with shock after a heavy crash-landing. Four weeks later he joined 70 Squadron in France. On one occasion his Sopwith Camel aircraft was badly damaged by anti-aircraft fire during a photographic reconnaissance mission.

On 5 August 1917, Budden found himself in a duel against German ace, Hermann Göring, as recorded in the book *Under the Guns of the German Aces* by Norman Franks and Hal Giblin: [15]

> [Göring's Jasta 27 squadron] ran into a patrol of Sopwith Camels from No. 70 Squadron. Göring picked out an opponent and attacked. The Camel's pilot seemed anxious to keep the fight above the trench lines and to avoid straying too far over the German side. Göring followed him closely, firing at a range of no more than 50 metres. According to Göring, flames began to come from the Sopwith and, trailing smoke, it went into a spin and was lost in a cloud. The Staffelführer was certain he had shot the Camel down and it seemed his judgement was vindicated when, on 29 August, he was officially credited with the victory.
>
> In fact, Göring's opponent was Lieutenant Gilbert Budden and although he was wounded in the combat and his machine badly damaged, he still managed to land the Camel near Bailleul.

It isn't known whether Gilbert found out who his opponent was that day, or what he thought as Hermann Göring rose to power during the 1930s with the Nazi Party in Germany, commanding the German Air Force during the Second World War. In stark contrast, Gilbert served in this second worldwide conflict as the Assistant County Secretary for the Red Cross in Cambridgeshire.

— — —

Despite the plans put forward in early 1916, it wasn't until 1923 that a permanent memorial to thirty-three of those from Hulme Hall who died during the war was installed in the Chapel. The story of how the memorial came to be was told in the 1922–1924 Hulme Hall Chronicle: [16]

On Sunday, March 18th, 1917, a Memorial Service was held for those who laid down their lives up to that date. Even before that the project had been brought forward of making some permanent Memorial, the precise form to be determined when it was found what sum of money was available for the purpose. Accordingly, an appeal was issued, and in 1923 it was felt that the time had come to close the appeal and to determine what should be done. A Mural Tablet in oak and bronze was found to be the most suitable permanent Memorial which the amount subscribed made it possible to erect. After deliberation it was decided to place this upon the wall at the west end of the present Chapel. It will be possible to remove it into the permanent Chapel when the time comes that the plans for this, made 20 years ago, can be carried out.

The Chairman of the Governing body, the Bishop of Manchester, kindly consented to dedicate the Tablet on Sunday, 26th October. The relatives of all whose names are on the Tablet were invited to be present. After the dedication the Bishop gave a short address, the substance of which was as follows:

The losses of the War have fallen most heavily on Societies like this. The young had necessarily been the chief victims. They had offered their all to defeat a movement towards a World Empire of Might and such a cause was "God's Cause".

Those members of the Hall, whom we commemorate to-day, gave their lives to gain the victory for "God's Cause". Not that all would have expressed in that explicit way the motives that animated them. They might even have denied God's Presence in the world. Still, whether they understood it so or not, they had been fighting for Right to be recognised in international affairs and not mere Might, and this was helped to hasten the coming of God's Kingdom. Therefore, it is fitting that their Memorial should be in the Hall Chapel, and it should remind us that the Cause for which they fell is not finally won. We had, what is perhaps the harder duty, of serving that Cause without the glory and excitement of an instant's decision, and with less exhilarating service of earnest effort in the common round of everyday life.

The reason why only thirty-three of the forty who died were added to the memorial is unclear. It may have been that the death of a former resident had not been reported to Hulme Hall staff, or the person may not have met a particular criteria set out by the committee who commissioned the memorial.

Of the 'missing' seven, Noel Gornell is the only student not to have studied at Hulme Hall. Noel had been awarded a Hulme Hall scholarship and should have started at Manchester in October 1917 but deferred, having received a commission with the Royal Engineers. Noel was killed in March 1918, with his death being reported in the Hulme Hall Chronicle.

Frank Caress, who first arrived at Hulme Hall in October 1910, died of illness in October 1918. Having enlisted with the 5th Battalion Cheshire Regiment in August 1914, Frank was discharged from the army on medical grounds in February 1915, only weeks before his friends and colleagues sailed to war. Although he could have returned to his work with the River Weaver Navigation Trustees, Frank instead chose to work as an engineer with the Atlantic Transport Line, on the SS *Irishman*, facing the threat of German submarines as he travelled to and from America.

William Warrington and Harry Farrimond both died as a result of illness in early 1919.

William Warrington was one of the original group of students who joined Hulme Hall when it reopened in 1887. A Captain in the Royal Army Medical Corps, he spent the war working at the 1st Western General Hospital in Liverpool.

Harry Farrimond entered Hulme Hall in October 1914, enlisting with the 20th Battalion Royal Fusiliers in 1915. He fought with the Royal Fusiliers on the Western Front before receiving a commission with the East Lancashire Regiment in 1917. Harry contracted malaria whilst serving in Salonika, Greece, which resulted in him being hospitalised on a number of occasions. Having died in 1919 after being discharged, it wasn't until October 1923, after a campaign by his mother, that the army acknowledged Harry's death was linked to the malaria he contracted whilst on active service.

Dudley Francis, Arthur Marshall and Thomas Fawsitt were all killed in action in France.

Dudley Francis entered Hulme Hall in October 1903 to study Engineering. Having only just turned sixteen years old, Dudley struggled with university life and was removed on the recommendation of the Warden in early 1904.

Arthur Marshall resided at Hulme Hall during the 1908-1909 academic year whilst undertaking a private Mathematics course in Manchester, before leaving to start a degree in Mechanical Science at Cambridge University.

Thomas Fawsitt was at Hulme Hall from October 1910 to study Medicine. However, his work ethic was not up to the standard expected and he left Hulme Hall in March 1911 on the request of the Warden.

Should the names of the 'missing' seven be added to the Hulme Hall War Memorial? This is debate that needs to be had. Regardless of whether the names of the seven are added to the Memorial, their stories are told in the latter section of this book as members of the Hulme Hall community.

THE GREAT WAR: 1914–1919

A short history of the First World War
Written by Ashley Hern

As with any publication on the First World War, or Great War as it was referred to by some at the time, it is important to provide some context to a conflict that grew from a political assassination in Sarajevo to a full-blown worldwide conflict within only a matter of months. It was a war that was to cost the lives of millions of soldiers and civilians and, despite hopes that it was to be 'the war that ended all wars', set in motion events that would lead to a second, more devastating world war only twenty years later.

This short introduction to the First World War is intended to assist the reader in understanding the background and some of the critical events of the conflict into which the men of Hulme Hall, and so many of their generation, were thrown.

1914

> He was in the OTC at school, and for one term at the University, which he left in December, 1914, receiving his commission in the 3rd Battalion (Special Reserve) Welsh Regiment in the following January.
>
> Throughout his active service he was always hopeful and cheerful, doing what he regarded as his privilege and duty in fighting the "Hun," whom he detested.
>
> *Extracts from an obituary of Arthur Lord, published in the Hulme Hall Chronicle. Arthur was at Hulme Hall between September and December 1914.* [17]

The assassination of Archduke Franz Ferdinand in Sarajevo on 28 June 1914 by the Serbian nationalist Gavrilo Princip was the catalyst through which past decades of rising tensions in Europe erupted into armed conflict. Geopolitical rivalry, ethnic nationalism and economic competition resulted in institutionalised mistrust and paranoia, which eroded the framework for international co-operation laid down at the Congress of Vienna in 1815. After diplomacy failed to resolve the subsequent July crisis, the main powers of Europe initiated their war plans.

Austro-Hungary invaded Serbia, whom it blamed for organising the assassination, on 28 July, an act which triggered the complex system of alliances and mutual defence pacts which were strung across the globe. In response to Russian moves to aid its fellow Slavs in Serbia, Germany invaded Belgium on 4 August 1914 as part of the Schlieffen Plan. This sought to achieve a quick victory over France by passing around the French defensive system on the Franco-German border and capturing Paris. Once this was achieved Germany would be able to focus its full attention onto France's ally, Russia, whose mobilisation was anticipated to take six weeks to complete on account of its vast size.

France invaded its former territories of Alsace-Lorraine on 7 September but its armies were quickly repulsed by the German defenders. The German plan was also unravelling as its advance through Belgium was slowed by dogged Belgian resistance, assisted by the arrival of the British Expeditionary Force (BEF). Britain had entered the war on the 4 August arguing that the Treaty of London (1839), committing it to defend Belgian neutrality, was still valid. In reality, Britain's main aim was to aid its French ally against an expansionist Germany, which posed a serious threat to British imperial power.

The BEF fought two brief but bloody encounters in Belgium with the German 1st Army (Mons being the most famous) before being forced to retreat. This turned out to be serendipitous as it exposed the limitations of the German commander, von Moltke. The higher than expected resistance created concern about his exposed army columns and he insisted that they concentrate more closely. This kept the German armies to the east of Paris and created an opportunity for the French to counter-attack, which they did on 5–12 September at the First Battle of the Marne. Attacked from both sides, aided by the Paris garrison who travelled to the front in city taxis, the Germans were themselves forced to retreat, but stopped on the north side of the Aisne, where they repulsed French and British attempts to dislodge them.

To avoid a stalemate, both sides clattered northwards in a disorganised rush attempting to outflank each other, an event that is usually dignified with the name 'Race to the Sea'. In the confused situation several battles occurred, most notably the First Battle of Ypres (19 October–22 November) which saw dangerous German attempts to break through the French, British and Belgian lines repulsed with great loss. All sides suffered significant casualties, as soldiers were exposed to the immense firepower of modern rifles, machine guns and artillery. Trenches were initially improvised affairs aimed at providing temporary cover before renewal of inevitable offensive warfare. Exhaustion and winter weather saw a halt to major operations by the end of November all across the new Western Front that ran from the English Channel to the Vosges. The trenches now became permanent and an institutionalised part of a new form of warfare.

Faced with a prolonged campaign, Britain recalled its forces stationed in imperial garrisons across the globe to be sent to fight in France. However, the conflict gained its global character almost immediately when the British decided that they needed to eliminate the German colonies in Africa. German Togoland surrendered quickly on 26 August in the face of a combined invasion by French and British forces. However, this was overshadowed by two disastrous military expeditions in southwest and eastern Africa. In September a South African expedition aimed at securing German Southwest Africa was defeated by the German Schutztruppen at the Battle of Sandfontein, which in turn triggered off a Boer rebellion against the Republic's decision to side with the British. In East Africa, an offensive into German East Africa led to a calamitous British defeat, when an amphibious attack at Tanga was driven back into the sea with most of their equipment abandoned on the beach. The German commander Paul von Lettow-Vorbeck would prove to be a resilient opponent who then proceeded to launch raids into British East Africa for the next eighteen months, delaying further British operations considerably.

1915

> It was the dreadful frontal assaults that laid our men in heaps. In the trenches one stands a reasonable chance of survival but once over the parapet and you are in the roll of honour.
>
> *Lieutenant Robert Bedford, Gallipoli – August 1915*
> *Hulme Hall 1912–1914* [18]

In 1915 the Western Allies planned a series of spring offensives in Artois with the French aiming to attack Vimy Ridge, whilst the British attacked further north. The French attack was cancelled whilst the British offensive at Neuve

Chapelle (10–13 March) achieved some initial successes but shortages of shells and a lack of co-ordination allowed the Germans to counter-attack. The Germans used chlorine gas at the start of the Second Battle of Ypres (22 April–25 May), which saw the creation of the Ypres Salient.

There was disagreement amongst the Allies over future strategy. The French wanted to expel the German forces from northern France as quickly as possible: not only was their presence an affront to French national pride, but the Germans controlled valuable natural resources which were being directed to support the German war effort. Britain had showed its commitment to the war by reversing its traditional strategy of minimal military involvement on the European mainland. Lord Kitchener, Minister of War, began a campaign to exploit the war fever of the summer of 1914, raising a 'New Army' of volunteers to compete with the continental conscript armies. However, there were those in the higher echelons of the British government who believed that the Western Front would not achieve a result, and that efforts should be expended elsewhere to achieve some victories that could help maintain high morale at home.

This led to the attempt to knock the Ottoman Empire out of the war by naval attack. After the failure of the naval offensive in March 1915 due to the tenacity of the Turkish defensive batteries, hurriedly assembled troops were landed on the Gallipoli peninsula on the 25 April to secure the entry to the straits. Poorly equipped and organised, the offensive soon bogged down in the face of resolute Turkish defence, and despite a renewal of the attack in August, trench warfare ensued at great cost and little advantage. The attack was called off in December.

In the Middle East the British attempted to push the Ottomans out of Mesopotamia, but this ended with the siege of Kut (December 1915-April 1916), where the British were forced to surrender to the Ottomans. These disasters strengthened the arguments of the 'westerners' in the British government who argued that the decisive action would take place on the Western Front and these other expeditions were distractions.

There was more success in German Southwest Africa where the largely South African Army led by Louis Botha and Johann Smuts managed to defeat the local German forces by July. East Africa remained a problem with the British slowly rebuilding their forces, whilst attempting to eliminate German naval assets in the area. The Germans continued to conduct raids into British controlled territory causing considerable alarm.

Units of Kitchener's new armies were deployed for the first time in the autumn offensives planned for 1915. The French attacks in Champagne and Artois in September were supported by a major attack by the British at Loos, as well as an Italian offensive against the Austro-Hungarians. Despite the first British use of poison gas, the Battle of Loos (25 September–14 October) failed to achieve any sustained result due to a failure to follow up initial successes with timely reinforcements. The Germans had been working to increase the depths of their defences over the previous year and Allied attacks were simply not powerful enough to overcome them. The Western Allies decided that they had to co-ordinate their activities more closely and representatives of the British, French, Russian and Italian high commands met at Chantilly on the 5 December.

1916

> My job is transport work. We take provisions and trench materials to the troop. Our work is behind the lines and not accompanied with the same risks as other units have to face. It becomes very monotonous at times – an occasional shelling keeps us alive; but the high explosive shell is not a pleasant neighbour.
>
> Lieutenant William Wildblood, Western Front – January 1916
> *Hulme Hall 1908–1909* [19]

In 1916 the Germans changed their strategy in the west to a more active one. The German chief-of-staff von Falkenhayen proposed a battle of attrition which would diminish the French Army's strength by forcing them into a series of costly offensives. Thus began the Battle of Verdun (February–December 1916), which saw extremely high casualties on both sides as the French desperately tried to defend the city whilst showing considerable initiative in resupplying and managing soldiers' morale whilst the German strategy miscarried and they suffered significantly higher losses than they anticipated.

In order to help relieve the pressure on the French, the new British commander Douglas Haig was ordered to prepare an Anglo-French offensive in the Somme region in the summer. The Somme Offensive (1 July–13 November) has proved controversial due to the high British casualties in the first days of fighting due to the failure of the initial week-long bombardment to destroy the well-designed German defences. However, the offensive was renewed several times over the next months, with tanks being used for the first time to little strategic effect in September 1916. The German policy of immediate counter-attack when losing positions meant that they suffered around 600,000 casualties compared with similar losses for the British and French. The combined losses of the Somme and Verdun battles were a major blow to German military capabilities in the long term as their losses were not as easy as the Allies' to replace.

In the Middle East the British finally managed to initiate an Arab revolt against the Ottomans using the plans laid down by T E Lawrence, as well as managing to protect the Suez Canal from Ottoman offensives. German Cameroon was surrendered to British forces in March 1916 after a long campaign that had begun in 1914. In East Africa the British Imperial forces invaded German territory in alliance with the Belgians in May, which gradually advanced into the hinterland. However, Belgian reluctance to advance further combined with reliance on motorised transport meant that it was impossible to obtain any decisive result against the German Schutztruppen. The German commander von Lettow deployed his native troops with great skill using their mobility, excellent bush craft and guerrilla tactics to slow down the Allied advances.

Although both sides had failed to achieve a breakthrough, the events of 1916 saw the Germans' overall strategic position weakened. Their Allies were still numerically superior and out-producing the Germans industrially. As a result, von Falkenhayen was sacked and replaced by von Hindenburg and his able executive officer Ludendorff in September. The failure of the German fleet to break the Allied blockade at the indecisive Battle of Jutland in the early summer was another major threat to German ability to continue the war economically.

1917

> Captain Harker dived down to 4000 feet after a hostile machine, the engine of which was damaged by the fire of Lieutenant Fernald, his observer. This machine finally landed in a field, as well as another Albatros, which had dropped out of the fight at the same time. As the air was by that time clear of the enemy, Captain Harker with great skill reformed the survivors.
>
> *Mention of Captain Howard Harker, Hulme Hall 1910–13, in the diary of 57 Squadron from April 1917 during the Battle of Arras.* [20]

The Brusilov Offensive in the summer of 1916 by the Russian armies on the Eastern Front had destroyed the opposing Austro-Hungarian force. This required significant reinforcements from Germany to stabilise a situation made even worse by Romania throwing in its lot with the British and French. In these circumstances Hindenburg and Ludendorff decided to place Germany on the strategic defensive in 1917, and use other means to achieve a positive result, especially after peace overtures were rejected by the Allies in December 1916. The German economy was brought under direct government control, and a defensive system called the Hindenburg Line was begun behind the extant German front lines in France. This would allow a shortening of the defended front, releasing men for offensives elsewhere. A return to the policy of unrestricted submarine warfare against all shipping headed towards Great Britain would cause economic problems and a strategic bombing offensive was planned to try to undermine civilian morale.

Whilst Allied discussions sought to continue the co-ordination of effort during 1916, the French commander Joffre was sacked in December and replaced by General Nivelle. He promised his government and soldiers a decisive breakthrough by deploying sophisticated artillery attacks. Joffre's reputation meant he had been held in high regard by the British and his removal weakened Allied co-operation. Before Nivelle's offensive could be launched the Germans withdrew from their more exposed frontlines towards the Hindenburg Line in February and March. Initial diversions by the British forces were relatively successful with the Battles of Arras (9 April–16 May 1917) and Vimy Ridge (9–12 April) both achieving significant early gains.

Despite lavish promises, the Nivelle Offensive along the Chemin des Dames (16 April–9 May) was a disaster as it failed to achieve the promised German collapse, and the French suffered much higher casualties than predicted. The French Army then suffered a series of mutinies which undermined its ability to function. Nivelle was sacked and the French Army was rebuilt under the guidance of Pétain, the new French commander. Fortunately, the Germans never realised the poor condition of the French Army and so failed to exploit the opportunity. Significantly, in April the USA entered the war on the Allied side, angered by the U-boat campaign which was sinking US ships and ham-fisted German attempts to get Mexico to enter the war on their side.

To divert German attention from the French collapse, Haig lobbied the new British Prime Minister Lloyd George to carry out his long-held plans for an offensive in the Ypres Salient to remove the Germans from their control of the high ground around the city. This was also designed to regain control of the Belgian coast and undermine the German U-boat campaign, as well as being part of a political struggle to keep the focus of the British war effort onto the Western Front. After the huge casualties of the Somme Offensive, Lloyd George was sceptical about the prospect of success in France, and wanted easier options in Italy or the Balkans to try to put pressure on Germany via Austro-Hungary.

The Third Battle of Ypres (31 July–10 November), or Passchendaele, saw the British gradually push the Germans back at significant cost, though they were impeded by the unseasonably heavy rainfall that turned the battlefield into a quagmire. The Germans had no answer to the 'bite and hold' techniques which the British had developed over the previous years, and they suffered significant casualties. However, whilst some progress was made, it was only a handful of miles and the Allies were no closer to capturing the Belgian coast. Haig's decision to continue the offensive at Passchendaele into November brought him more criticism than the Somme. Haig was forced to cancel the offensive earlier than he intended as reinforcements were rushed to Italy to prevent a collapse after the huge defeat inflicted by the Austro-German forces at Caporetto in October/November.

In an attempt to maintain the pressure on the Germans a combined arms attack using tanks, artillery and infantry was launched at Cambrai (20 November–7 December) which achieved stunning success at first, However, failure to support the tanks effectively with infantry meant that the Germans were able to first stop the tanks, then successfully counter-attack. This battle laid the pattern for many of the battles in 1918.

In East Africa Smuts prematurely declared victory on his departure in January 1917, but a series of poor strategic decisions by a revolving door of successors allowed the numerically inferior German forces to continue their mobile campaign, greatly frustrating British attempts to trap them, and inflicting considerable casualties. By the end of the year von Lettow abandoned German East Africa and took what was left of his forces south into Portuguese East Africa aiming to continue his strategy of tying down as many British forces as possible and weakening their deployments in France.

1918

> Shortly after reaching the canal an enemy plane came over bombing and got three direct hits in the canal killing 2/Lt W F Williams and 3 Other Ranks
>
> *The death of Second Lieutenant William Fredrick Williams, Hulme Hall, 1915–1918, on the Canal du Nord near Cambrai in September 1918, as reported in the War Diaries of the 17th Battalion Royal Fusiliers* [21]

The German Army had suffered overstretch in 1917 responding to the Allied attacks and their strategy of defence was nullified by being forced to expend irreplaceable reserves in patching up their defences. With the imminent arrival of the first American troops in France, the German high command decided they need to go onto the offensive to put them in as strong a position as possible before peace negotiations began. Fortunately, the fighting on the Eastern Front had died down in 1917, with the March revolution in Russia, partially caused by war-weariness, undermining Russian attempts to continue fighting. The seizure of power in November by the Bolsheviks brought the war in the east to an end and the Germans gained huge swathes of land in the Ukraine and Byelorussia under the provisions of the treaty of Brest-Litovsk signed in March 1918. This freed up nearly one million troops who were moved west to help launch a series of attacks in the spring, known collectively as the Ludendorff Offensive (21 March–18 July). This consisted of four main offensives that aimed to drive the British back to the English Channel and destroy them, thus forcing the French to come to terms with the Germans.

Using new tactics, the best German soldiers were given new weapons and formed into 'Stormtrooper' divisions that infiltrated the Allied front lines leaving defensive strong-points for support troops to capture. This led to some spectacular advances and much of the territory seized by the Allies during the fighting in 1916 and 1917 was lost in a matter of weeks. However, Ludendorff's strategy was not coherent: the Stormtroopers quickly ran out of their supplies and the follow-up forces often suffered heavy casualties when they attacked the remaining strong-points. The British and French were able to organise a stressful but coherent retreat and by May 1918 the position had stabilised, though the Germans persisted in attacking until July.

In August, with American divisions pouring into France, the Allies began a series of offensives known as the Hundred Days (8 August–11 November).

Under the co-ordinating guidance of the French commander Foch, the British and French used their experience to launch combined arms attacks of precise artillery bombardments followed up by tanks and infantry, supported by aircraft. The German Army, severely depleted by the spring offensives, was forced back and when the armistice was signed on 11 November the Germans were almost completely expelled from France and being forced back into eastern Belgium and Luxembourg.

1919

> The raging desire still continues to be demobilised quickly. Nevertheless, I feel pretty sure that, for many, there will be pathetic disillusionment.
>
> In the trenches, the troops have had plenty of time for thought, and, as 'Happy Days' said the other day, there has grown up in their minds a heavenly picture of an England which does not exist, and never did exist, and never will exist so long as men are human.
>
> After all, there was a good deal to be said in favour of the old trench life. There were none of the mean haunting fears of poverty there, and the next meal – if you were alive to take it – was as certain as the rising sun. The rations were the same for the 'haves' and the 'have nots', and the shells fell, without favour, upon both.
>
> In spite – or partly perhaps because of the gloominess of the surroundings – there was an atmosphere of selflessness and a spirit of camaraderie the like of which has probably not been seen in the world before, at least on so grand a scale. Such is the influence of the shells!
>
> *Lieutenant Colonel Rowland Fielding, writing to his wife in February 1919. Fielding was resident at Hulme Hall from September 1888 whilst studying for a degree in Engineering at the university, and survived the War having served on the Western Front for over four years.* [22]

The victorious world powers met in Paris from the 18 January 1919 and tried to establish a peace settlement that would prevent the bloodshed of the past years happening again. With the world plagued by economic collapse, Spanish influenza and political turmoil, the idealism of Woodrow Wilson was increasingly tempered by the Great Power pragmatism of France and Great Britain. Whilst the League of Nations was set up as a forum for resolving future disputes, France and Great Britain were able to impose a punitive settlement on Germany, blaming her for the war and demanding compensation in the form of financial reparations. The old empires of western Eurasia, Austro-Hungary, the Ottoman Empire, Germany and Russia all disappeared to be replaced by a series of compromise nation states that recognised some cases of ethnic self-determination, whilst denying others; a legacy that still plagues the world today. Although it ultimately contributed to the Second World War, and was roundly condemned by some participants, given the circumstances historians would argue that the Paris Conference did achieve some remarkable results.

A SUPREME AND INCORRUPTIBLE TREASURE

The lives and deaths of the men who failed to return

It is a rule of the Hall Chronicle that we shall not speak praise of one another, but death may release us. A Major of the Manchester Territorials wrote thus of Freemantle: 'He was shot successively through both arms but still went forward though quite paralysed. He directed work in the trench, breaking a tooth by clenching his teeth with pain. Finally he was shot through the body. He was utterly fearless.'

Rev J H Hopkinson in a letter to past and present Hulme Hall residents, January 1916 published in the 1914–1915 Hulme Hall Chronicle [23]

SECTION 1

Hulme Hall men who were killed or died during the First World War and are remembered on the War Memorial

The accounts of the men are ordered according to the date they arrived at Hulme Hall

Major

ERNEST NICHOLSON CUNLIFFE, OBE

Royal Army Medical Corps

Hulme Hall Resident No. 135
Died of Illness 1919

Born	5 November 1877
Date Entered Hulme Hall	October 1896
Degree Course	Medicine
Regiment	Royal Army Medical Corps
Awards	OBE; Mentioned in Dispatches
Died of Illness	31 March 1919
Age	41
Buried	St Mary's, Windermere, England

Pre-War

Ernest Nicholson Cunliffe was born in 1877 in Bolton. Beginning his schooling at Bolton High School, he later attended Monmouth Grammar School before being accepted at Owens College, Manchester, in 1896 to study Medicine. Awarded a Hulme Hall Scholarship, Ernest, who was known as Peter amongst his friends, started what would become a close and long association with Hulme Hall.

Gifted both academically and athletically, Ernest graduated in 1901 with First Class Honours. During his time as a student he was captain of the University Rugby 1st XV and was awarded university colours for athletics, running in both the 440 yards and mile events. He could also be found playing in most inter-hall sports events and was particularly renowned for his successes at tennis and fives. Upon graduating, Ernest continued to reside at Hulme Hall, taking on the role of Medical Tutor.

Impressed with his organising ability, in 1906 he was elected to the honorary staff by the Board of Management of the Manchester Royal Infirmary. In June 1911 he married Harriet Clegg at High Compton, near Oldham.

War Service

Ernest held a commission in the Royal Army Medical Corps (RAMC) at the outbreak of the war and was on the staff of the 2nd Western General Hospital based in Manchester. The following edited text has been taken from an obituary published in the 1916–1920 edition of the Hulme Hall Chronicle: [24]

> Cunliffe was soon appointed Registrar with the rank of Major and threw himself with tremendous energy into the work. His genius for administration was soon evident and this, combined with his capacity for hard work, contributed in no small measure to the building up of the huge organisation which such a large general hospital needed. Day after day, including Sundays, and often into the night, Cunliffe could be seen steadily ploughing his way through piles of papers and documents in his office at Whitworth Street. Only those who have worked what was practically double time in a large office of this kind can realise the incessant strain of administrative work such as fell to his lot.

The merit of his work was recognised when the Commanding Officer left to go on service in France, for Cunliffe was then made Commanding Officer and promoted to Lieutenant Colonel. After six months in command he went on active service to France and served there until he was recalled to take command again. In France he was freed from administrative duties and was able to show the other sides of his character which had previously endeared him to those who knew him at the Hall and in his student life. He left behind him a record of genial friendship and of athletic prowess and his departure was much regretted by all who had learned to know him well.

On his return to Manchester he settled down at once to hard and unremitting toil in the office and this, coming immediately after his six months of open-air life in France, no doubt had a great deal to do with developing the illness which proved fatal. In spite of failing health and frequent headaches which often made work very trying for him, he held on with very little holiday until an attack of influenza made it impossible for him to continue. This was followed by a long and painful illness and in the spring of 1919 the 2nd Western General hospital lost a revered and beloved Commanding Officer. The award of a Military OBE was an honour richly deserved.

'No word of Cunliffe's life and character is complete without a reference to his family life. He was an ideal husband and father and our sympathy goes out to his wife and children in their irreparable loss. Those of us who saw the devotion of his wife to him during the four years of strain when he was over-working know how great was her part in sustaining him and enabling him to make the efforts he made.' [24]

Second Lieutenant
ARTHUR CYRIL RICHARDS DAVIES

North Stafford Regiment

Hulme Hall Resident No. 213
Died of Illness 1915

Born	13 October 1885
Date Entered Hulme Hall	October 1903
Degree Course	Engineering
Regiment	5th Battalion North Stafford Regiment
Died of Illness	27 October 1915
Age	30
Buried	St Cadoc Churchyard, Trevethin, Monmouthshire, Wales

Pre-War

Arthur Cyril Richards was born in Trevethin, Wales, in 1885 to William and Sarah Davies. William worked as a Mechanical Engineer.

After completing his secondary education at Monmouth Grammar School, Arthur was accepted on the Engineering course at Owens College in 1903. Finding the degree not quite as expected, he left and enrolled onto a private engineering course but continued to reside at Hulme Hall.

He left Manchester in 1906 to work with his father who was the General Manager at the Shelton Iron, Steel & Coal Company's Works in Sheffield. After his father died in 1913, Arthur continued to work with the company as an Assistant Engineer until August 1914.

War Service

Arthur volunteered with the 5th North Staffordshire Regiment at the outbreak of war. Training initially in Stoke, the Battalion transferred to Luton where they continued training for active service whilst being quartered in a variety of schools and straw-hat factories.

In December they were moved to Essex. By now, Arthur's leadership qualities evidently had come to the fore and he was promoted from Private to Second Lieutenant in February. One month later, the Battalion were mobilised to France.

Upon arrival, the Battalion stayed in a rest camp for a couple of days before enjoying a train ride across France to the border with Belgium from where they had a 25km march, ending the day sleeping in field near Estaires. They awoke the next morning to the sounds of an armoured train firing its array of guns nearby. Soon afterwards the Battalion were met by parties of wounded men walking back from the trenches who had been involved in the Battle of Neuve Chapelle. The procession lasted all day.

At the beginning of April, the Battalion took over a section of front-line trenches approximately six miles from Ypres. The enemy trench was extremely close; at most between 50 to 300 yards away. A 'positive' of being so close to the enemy was that there was very little shelling, with both sides concerned about hitting their own men. A significant disadvantage was that the slightest exposure above the trench was likely to result in being shot by a sniper.

Arthur would spend four days serving in the front line and four days in reserve. On 24 April Arthur became the first officer casualty in the Battalion when he was struck by a German bullet in the back of his left knee, fracturing his kneecap. Having been rushed to the nearest aid station, Arthur was evacuated to England the next day on the hospital ship the *St Patrick*.

By September 1915 the wound was still causing Arthur trouble but it was generally expected that he would fully recover. An Army Medical Board assembled on 29 September and recommended that it would only be a month before Arthur could resume light duties in England, and four months before he would be fit for general service. However only four weeks later, he developed appendicitis and died after an operation at Kidderminster Infirmary.

During his time with the Battalion, Arthur and his colleagues might have been one of the most frequently inspected Battalions in the army. In September 1914 they were inspected by Lord Kitchener. Before being sent to France they were inspected by King George V in February, just after Arthur had been promoted. Whilst Arthur was serving on the Western Front, the Battalion were also inspected by both Field Marshal Sir John French and the Bishop of London on separate occasions. [25]

Private

HAROLD DANBY SWIFT

Australian Imperial Force

Hulme Hall Resident No. 228
Killed in Action 1917

Born	7 January 1885
Date Entered Hulme Hall	October 1904
Degree Course	Matriculation Course
Regiment	15th Battalion Australian Imperial Force
Killed in Action	28 August 1917, Messines Ridge
Age	32
Commemorated	Menin Gate, Ypres, Belgium

Pre-War

Harold was born in Sheffield in 1885 to Harry and Grace Swift.

Harold attended Ackworth School in Pontefract, which was founded by Quakers in 1779. Once he finished school, he was accepted at Victoria University of Manchester to undertake a matriculation course which he started in October 1904, staying at Hulme Hall.

Struggling academically, he left university in June 1905 having not completed the course. Harold headed back to Sheffield where he found a job as a clerk at a local steel works, working alongside his father who was a manager at the same plant.

In January 1912 Harold emigrated to Australia, leaving the UK for Sydney on the White Star Liner *Runic*. By 1914 he was working as a groom in Murwillumbah, New South Wales.

War Service

Harold attempted to join the Australian Imperial Force on a number of occasions at the outbreak of war, initially being rejected due to his height (Harold was 5'3") and the condition of his teeth. As casualties began to mount rapidly, and the demand for reinforcements increased, the medical and physical standards required by the Australian Army were relaxed. In November 1916, with height restrictions lowered and the medical team turning a blind eye to his teeth, Harold was declared medically fit and enlisted into the Australian Army.

In December 1916 he married Muriel Field just six weeks before boarding the *SS Ayrshire* to begin a four-month journey to England.

In May 1917, having only just landed in England, Harold went absent without leave (AWOL), returning to his training camp in Codford nine days later. Arrested and court marshalled, Harold was sentenced to eight days of Field Punishment No.2 (heavy labour duties) and docked eighteen days' pay. It isn't known why Harold went AWOL. Given that this was his first time back in England for over four years, and perhaps aware of the slim chance he had of coming back from war alive, it is thought likely that he travelled to Sheffield to spend time with his mother.

In mid-July Harold was sent to France to join the 4th Australian Depot.

Here Harold managed to get himself into trouble again, this time being charged with relieving himself in a public place; an offence that resulted in the loss of one day's pay.

From the depot, Harold was posted to the 15th Australian Infantry Battalion (AIB) on 11 August. He joined C Company whilst they were being held in support to Battalions in the front-line trenches at Messines Ridge. Harold's Battalion were responsible for providing work parties to repair sections of both the front-line and support trenches which had been damaged by the wet weather and enemy artillery fire.

On the evening of 28 August, the Battalion were relieved from duty in the reserve lines by the 16th Battalion Manchester Regiment. Under heavy artillery fire, Harold and his platoon were the last to move out and as they were making their way through the communication trenches Harold was struck by a shell. The shell subsequently exploded amongst the platoon, killing him instantly and severely wounding two of his friends.

Details of Harold's marriage weren't updated in his service records and his mother remained listed as next-of-kin. Harold's wife only found out about her husband's death a month after he was killed when reading the casualty lists published in an Australian newspaper. [26]

Second Lieutenant

GODFREY HAMILTON HEMSLEY

Canadian Field Ambulance
Royal Field Artillery

Hulme Hall Resident No. 237
Killed in Action 1917

Born	31 March 1886
Date Entered Hulme Hall	October 1905
Degree Course	Ordinary BSc
Regiment	10th Canadian Field Ambulance / Royal Field Artillery
Killed in Action	12 October 1917, Passchendaele
Age	31
Buried	Vlamertinghe New Military Cemetery, Belgium

Pre-War

Godfrey Hamilton was born in Lincoln in 1886, the fifth child to George and Rebecca Hemsley. George Hemsley was a music teacher and a Lay Vicar at Lincoln Cathedral.

Godfrey was educated at Lincoln Grammar School and in October 1905 went into residency at Hulme Hall having been awarded a scholarship to undertake an Ordinary BSc degree studying at the Victoria University of Manchester Day Training College. Unfortunately, he failed in his examinations at the end of course and he left both the university and Hulme Hall in 1908.

After leaving Hulme Hall, Godfrey taught at a school in Hyde before proceeding to The Hague where he held a post as foreign correspondent for four years. In April 1914 he emigrated to Canada to begin a career in farming.

War Service

Still a dominion of Great Britain in 1914, Canada's foreign policy was dictated by the British Government. As a result, Canada automatically declared war with Germany when Britain commenced hostilities on 4 August.

Given his adventurous nature, it is not surprising that Godfrey was one of the first to volunteer for the newly formed Canadian Expeditionary Force (CEF), but to his immense frustration he was rejected on the grounds of his poor eyesight.

Despite the setback, Godfrey applied to join the CEF a further seven times until he was finally accepted, over a year later, in September 1915 into the Canadian Field Ambulance Service. Having either found a sympathetic doctor, or mastered the format of the eye test, his sign-up papers suspiciously reveal that he had near perfect eyesight!

After six months of training in Canada, Godfrey arrived back in England in March 1916. On arrival at Bramshott, in Hampshire, he was promoted to the rank of Staff Sergeant and assigned as Quartermaster Sergeant for the 10th Battalion Canadian Field Ambulance (CFA).

Less than a month later, Godfrey and the 10th Battalion CFA were mobilised to Poperinghe, in Belgium, to support the British and Commonwealth Forces holding the front line at Ypres.

With a desire to take an active role in fighting at the outbreak of war, Godfrey would have found life as a Quartermaster Sergeant far from satisfying. As the year progressed, he applied, and was accepted, for training with the Royal Field Artillery. That the RFA medics picked up on Godfrey's poor eyesight, yet accepted him for officer training, demonstrates that the army was in need of men and were willing to relax the high standard of fitness in place when he first applied in 1914.

In March 1917 Godfrey crossed back to England to undertake five months of training, being commissioned as a Second Lieutenant in the British Army. On his return to Ypres, he was posted to C Battery of the 255th Brigade Royal Field Artillery as a Forward Observation Officer (FOO), responsible for coordinating fire onto a specific target.

And it was in this role of a FOO that Godfrey found himself operating in on 12 October 1917, at the start of the first assault on the village of Passchendele, part of the wider series of attacks later known as the Third Battle of Ypres. During the fighting, Godfrey was caught by the blast of an enemy shell and killed.

During his time as a Quartermaster Sergeant in France, Godfrey found himself arrested and charged with being drunk on active service. Defending himself during the subsequent court-marshal, Godfrey demonstrated that the claims against him were false, pointed out to the court neither the NCO who laid the charge, nor his senior on whose instructions the charge was laid, had been called by the prosecution. In fact both were off base at the time of the alleged incident. Godfrey was found not guilty.[27]

Lance Corporal

JOSEPH PERCIVAL MAIDEN

(Inniskilling) Dragoons

Hulme Hall Resident No. 262
Killed in Action 1917

Born	16 May 1889
Date Entered Hulme Hall	October 1907
Course	Teaching Certificate
Regiment	6th Battalion (Inniskilling) Dragoons
Killed in Action	1 December 1917
Age	28
Commemorated	Cambrai Memorial, Louverval, France

Pre-War

Joseph was born in Burslem, near Stoke-on-Trent. His father died when he was young leaving his wife, Maria, a teacher, to bring up Joseph and his brother Bertram.

Joseph attended the Potteries Pupil Teaching Centre where he undertook an apprenticeship as a pupil-teacher. The pupil-teacher system was introduced in 1846 with students undertaking a five-year apprenticeship, typically from the age of thirteen. Student teachers received instruction in teaching and were able to earn a wage working at primary schools.

Having completed his apprenticeship, Joseph entered Hulme Hall in 1907 to study for a Teaching Certificate at the University Day Training College. Here Joseph studied academic subjects as well as courses on the profession of teaching, such as the history and philosophy of education, and educational administration.

Joseph failed his exams in 1910 but passed in 1912 having spent the two years in between working on the staff at the Fielden Demonstration School in Manchester, a school set up by the university to enable students to put into practice in a controlled environment all that they were learning. By this stage, Joseph had left Hulme Hall and was staying with his uncle in Moss Side. Awarded his teaching certificate in October 1912, he left to teach at the newly opened Waterloo and Seaforth Grammar School. At some point between 1913 and August 1914, Joseph left teaching and started a career in journalism.

War Service

Having served in the University OTC whilst in Manchester, Joseph was quick to enlist to fight after war was declared, signing up as a Private with the Dragoon Guards in Liverpool on 11 September 1914. Towards the end of the month, he was posted to the 2nd Reserve Regiment of Cavalry who had been formed in August 1914 and were at that time based in Aldershot.

After almost eight months of training, Joseph was posted in May 1915 to the 6th Battalion (Inniskilling) Dragoons who been fighting on the Western Front since December. He served with distinction, being appointed to the rank of Lance Corporal just under a year later. On the evening of 14 August 1916, he was supervising a digging party ordered at night to undertake the construction of trenches near Neuville St Vaast, four miles to the north of Arras. The enemy were alert and fired upon Joseph and his colleagues, wounding him in the right thigh. He was evacuated back to England six days later to receive further treatment.

It took eight months to fully recover from the gunshot wound and on 30 April 1917 Joseph returned to his regiment who were now based in Thièvres, near Albert, on the Somme.

Seven months later, the 6th Dragoons were involved in the British offensive known as the Battle of Cambrai which started on 20 November 1917. Despite a successful and encouraging start, an enemy counter-attack starting at the end of November resulted in the British losing ground and taking heavy casualties. On 1 December, Joseph was involved in a failed cavalry charge which was to wound or kill 110 men and 187 horses from the Battalion.

Joseph was reported as Missing in Action with it later being ascertained that he had died of his wounds later that day having been taken prisoner by the Germans after the attack.

In 1922, Maria Maiden contacted the Cavalry Records Office to query why her late son's three war medals were stamped with the rank Private, not Corporal – a rank she believed he had been promoted to prior to returning to France in April 1917. The Records Office searched Joseph's records and replied that they could not find any trace of him being promoted to Corporal. They confirmed that Joseph had been appointed to 'Unpaid Lance Corporal' in April 1916 and 'Paid Lance Corporal' in February 1917. As the rank of Lance Corporal was an appointment, not a promotion, the rank of Private shown on Joseph's medals was confirmed as being correct. [28]

Lieutenant

WILLIAM GEORGE FREEMANTLE

Manchester Regiment

Hulme Hall Resident No. 263
Killed in Action 1915

Born	22 September 1889
Date Entered Hulme Hall	October 1907
Degree Course	Chemistry
Regiment	7th Battalion Manchester Regiment
Killed in Action	4 June 1915, Gallipoli
Age	25
Commemorated	Helles Memorial, Gallipoli

Pre-War

William was born in 1889 in Newbury, the second child of three to William and Louisa Freemantle.

After completing his primary education in Thatcham, William attended Sidcot School in Somerset where he was notable for his interest in photography and for taking the role of Laboratory Curator – both indicative of his interest in the sciences. It was therefore no surprise when he entered Hulme Hall in October 1907, to study Chemistry at the university.

It was during his time at Hulme Hall that William became heavily involved in the OTC. In 1909 he completed a course at the Hythe School of Musketry, and in the same year won the Major Thornburn Challenge Cup for general efficiency. A popular person with an outgoing personality, he became secretary of the OTC club, attained the rank of Quartermaster Sergeant.

Having successfully completed his degree in 1910, William found employment working as a chemical analyst with the Manchester Corporation Sewage Works in Davyhulme. He maintained an active role with the OTC and was an Officer with the 7th Battalion of the Manchester Regiment Territorial Force.

War Service

William could not wait to go to war. On holiday at his parents' in Newbury in August 1914, Lieutenant Freemantle was recalled to the 7th Battalion Manchester Regiment at the end of the month in order to prepare for active service abroad.

Initially posted to Khartoum in Sudan, William's enthusiasm may have waned slightly as the Battalion found themselves protecting British interests in the region rather than engaging the enemy.

In April 1915 all that changed when the Battalion were ordered to Cairo, where they joined with other units of the East Lancashire Territorial Division. On 3 May they embarked onto the SS *Ionian*, landing four days later in Gallipoli on the evening of 7 May at 'V' Beach, Cape Helles. Within a month, William would be killed in action during the Manchester Regiment's first serious assault of the campaign on 4 June. Fellow Officer W J Screwright wrote to William's parents to explain the circumstances of their son's death:[29]

I happened to be quite close to him just after we had taken the enemy's first line trench on 4 June. He was about the last Officer left of his Company, and was carrying on quite coolly under a terrific fire, and continued to do so a long time after he had been wounded in both arms, and not allowing anyone to touch him. When he met his death, it was instantaneous.

William's death highlighted a tragic shortfall in the War Office's communication to the parents of fallen soldiers. Given the terrible casualties suffered across several Manchester Regiments during the attacks of 4 June, it is not a surprise that the local Manchester newspapers were quick to publish news of the failed attacks. William's parents learned of the attack from these papers, and due to a misunderstanding saw that their son had been wounded, only to receive a telegram from the War Office shortly afterwards confirming that he had been killed in action.

'[Freemantle] was the life and soul of the many social gatherings held in connection with corps [Officer Training Corps], and spared no effort in making them a success.

Shortly after mobilising, speaking to an Evening News *reporter, [Freemantle] said, "Anyone can be sorry about this war, but if I have to leave the army after it is over, I don't care how long it lasts." No man was more delighted when orders for mobilisation were issued. He was only a little man, but he bubbled over with energy.'* [30]

1913-1914 University Rugby 1st XV – Christie Shield Winners
Aubrey Harris (middle row first left), Stephen Fisher (middle row second left) and Wilfred Treveylan (middle row third left) were regulars in the University 1st XV Rugby team during the 1913/14 season. Courtesy of The University of Manchester.

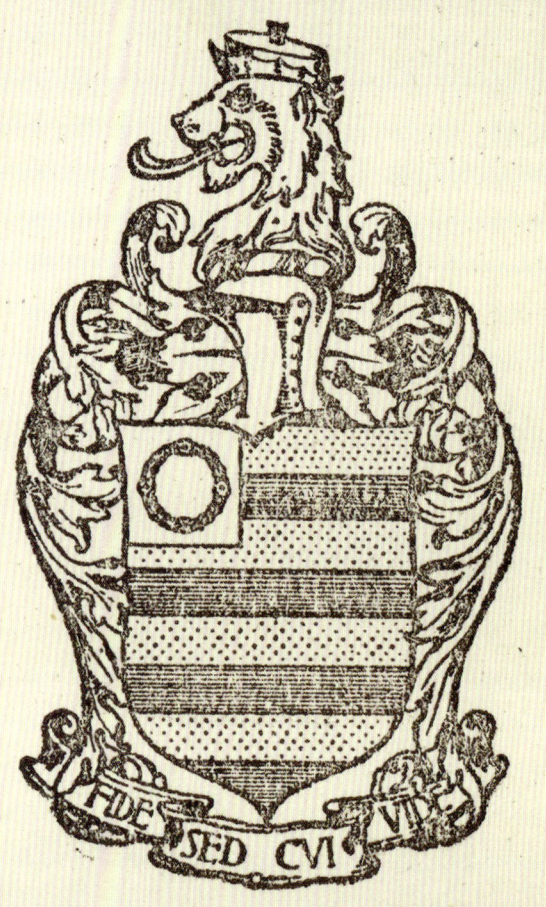

Hulme Hall Junior Common Room
Where was the Junior Common Room in 1914? The Author thinks it may have been the Old Dinning Room but is happy to be corrected. Courtesy of The University of Manchester.

Hulme Hall Crest circa 1910s
The Hulme Hall crest shown is said to have been designed by William Orlando Jones who studied Architecture at the University, entering Hall in 1910. Courtesy of The University of Manchester.

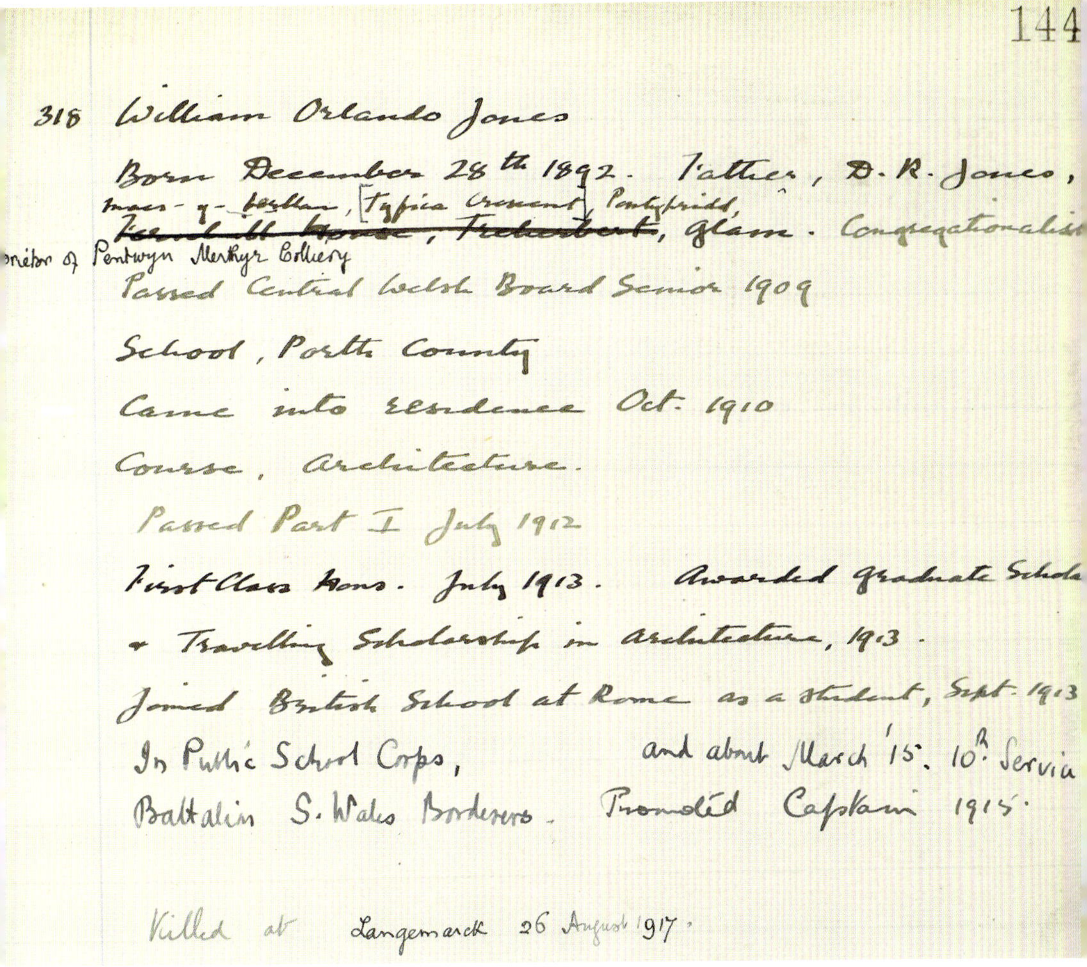

318 William Orlando Jones

Born December 28th 1892. Father, D. R. Jones, ~~mees-y-beglen~~, Typica Crescent, Pontypridd, ~~Kennedy House, Treherbert~~, Glam. Congregationalist, proprietor of Pentwyn Merthyr Colliery

Passed Central Welsh Board Senior 1909

School, Porth County

Came into residence Oct. 1910

Course, Architecture.

Passed Part I July 1912

First Class Hons. July 1913. Awarded Graduate Scholar + Travelling Scholarship in Architecture, 1913.

Joined British School at Rome as a student, Sept. 1913

In Public School Corps, and about March 15. 10th Service Battalion S. Wales Borderers. Promoted Captain 1915.

Killed at Langemarck 26 August 1917.

Page from Hulme Hall Administration Records

The Hulme Hall Administration records provided a rich source of information on students' backgrounds. This is William Orlando Jones' entry. Courtesy of The University of Manchester.

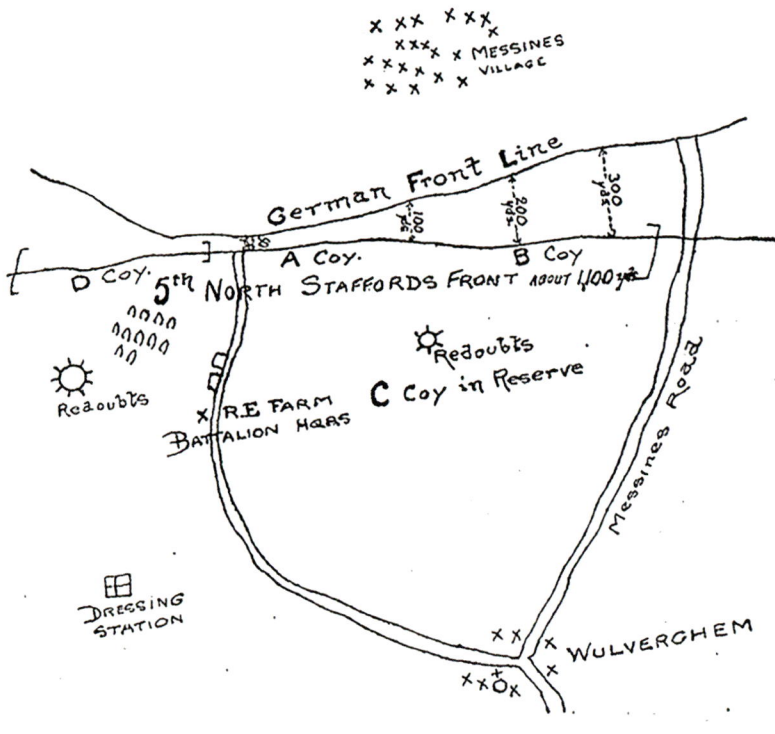

Map of trenches

Arthur Davies was wounded when rotating out of front line trenches in April 1915. The sketch of the trenches shows how close the 5th Battalion North Stafford Regiment was to the German Army; the gap between trenches was only 45m in places. Courtesy of the Staffordshire Regiment Museum.[69]

Davies family memorial

Arthur Davies was buried at the family grave in St Cadoc Churchyard, Trevethin, Monmouthshire in October 1915. Tragically Arthur was the third brother to die in the space of four months. John was killed in Gallipoli in June 1915 whilst Henry was killed in action at Loos in the same month as Arthur died. Author's own collection.

Please let me know if number seven three nought six pt harold danby swift killed in action three hundred thirtyninth casualty list is correct if so why was his wife not informed

Muriel Swift

Telegram from Muriel Swift

Copy of a telegram from Harold Swift's wife, Muriel, to the Australian War Office. Muriel only first heard about Harold's death having seen his name in a newspaper article a month after he was killed in action. National Archives of Australia (NAA: B2455, Swift, Harold Danby).

WOUNDED.

Lieutenant W. G. Freemantle, of the 7th Manchesters, is reported wounded. He went to his battalion from the University Officers' Training Corps. He was extremely popular with his brother officers, and had much to do in the times of peace with securing success for many social meetings of members of the O.T.C.

Manchester Evening News articles
William Freemantle's parents would have been relieved to hear that their son was wounded, as reported in the Manchester Evening News, on 11 June 1915 (above). Unfortunately the news was a mistake – William had been killed in action on 4 June during failed attacks at Gallipoli, with the error only being rectified in the same paper on 16 June (below). Image © Trinity Mirror. Image created courtesy of THE BRITISH LIBRARY BOARD

7th MANCHESTERS.

Six More Casualties Among Officers.

Lieutenant Freemantle Killed.

The 7th Battalion Manchester Regiment, like the other two Territorial Battalions which have their headquarters in Manchester, have apparently seen some more fierce fighting at the Dardanelles, as another batch of officers is reported to have fallen.

Information has been received to-day that no fewer than five officers have been wounded, while another, previously stated to have been wounded, is unfortunately now reported to have been killed.

Up to the present, as far as can be ascertained, the battalion has lost five officers killed and ten wounded.

The latest casualties are as under:
Lieutenant W. G. Freemantle, previously reported wounded, now reported killed.
Lieutenant G. Chadwick, wounded.
Lieutenant F. C. Palmer, wounded.
Lieutenant G. C. Hans Hamilton, wounded.
Lieutenant M. Norbury, wounded.
Lieutenant D. Norbury, wounded.

Kenneth Barry

Kenneth Barry grew up wanting to work in the textile industry. He was reluctant to stop studying to enlist but hoped the war would soon be over so he could continue in his chosen career. Supplied by Ronald Barry.

Christmas card
William Wildblood wrote a number of letters to Professor Tout, including a Christmas card in 1916, from the front line. Supplied by University of Manchester/ Cedric Wildblood/Alan Wildblood

William Wildblood and family
The photo of William (front row, far right) was taken at the Wildblood family home in Grimsby in the summer of 1916. William is with his father and mother (front row, far left and back row, left respectively), grandmother (front row, centre) and uncle (back row, right). Supplied by Cedric Wildblood/Alan Wildblood.

B.E.F.
France. 13/5/16.

Dear Prof. Tout,

I feel I must write after noticing in the paper that Pickles had been killed in action not very far from here. Soon after he came out perhaps 3 months ago I met him quite by accident in old "Pop" & took him to our mess for lunch. He was rather boyishly excited over his new experiences & I spent a very pleasant hour or two with him before he had to go — he was then just going on a bomb course. I tried to meet him when he was returning but at the camp I was told he was not back & immediately afterwards his regiment left. We followed to a place not very far away & as soon as I get an opportunity I shall try & get into touch with his regiment & find out any particulars I can. If you have heard anything yourself I should be very glad to hear from you. I feel that the History School has suffered a heavy loss & personally I find my thoughts keep on returning to the intercourse we had together. Not long since one of my colleagues at Colston's, a Captain in the Terriers, was killed in Mesopotamia.

Yours Sincerely,
W. W. Wildblood.

Letter from William Wildblood

William Wildblood had just heard of the death of his friend, and fellow Hulme Hall student, Harry Pickles when writing to Professor Tout in May 1916. Courtesy of The University of Manchester/Cedric Wildblood.

Robert and Winnie Southward
Robert with his sister Winnie. Date of the photo in unknown. Supplied by Donna Merrill.

Group photo of training soldiers
Robert Southward (bottom row, far right) during training. Robert received less than five months of training before he found himself in France. Supplied by Donna Merrill.

Sulby Mills
Sulby, I.O.M.
Oct. 17th 1916

Dear Mr. Nicklin,

I cannot tell you how your kind letter of sympathy was appreciated by my parents and myself. Robert's death has indeed been a terrible blow to us all and even yet it seems hard to realize it. As yet we have had very few particulars concerning his death.

Letter to Rev. Nicklin
The first page of a letter written to the Rev. Nicklin, the Hulme Hall Warden, by Winnie Southward following the death of her brother. Courtesy of The University of Manchester/ Donna Merrill

George Hebblethwaite as a student
Supplied by Deb Walker.

George Hebblethwaite at training
Lance Corporal George Hebblethwaite (centre) at training in late 1914 with the Duke of Wellington (West Riding) Regiment. Supplied by Deb Walker.

George Hebblethwaite – officer

After two months fighting on the Western Front, George returned to England to undertake officer training. Posted to the Lancashire Fusiliers after receiving a commission, he returned to France in June 1916. Supplied by Deb Walker.

Extracts from Upper Hopton Parish Magazine

Reported as 'Missing in Action' on 7 July 1916, George's family had to wait six weeks before he was confirmed to have been killed. Supplied by Hugh Baker/ Mirfield Team Parish.

UPPER HOPTON
PARISH MAGAZINE.

No 44.   AUGUST, 1916.   Price ONE PENNY

We are glad to see Captain Willie Marriott and are all so sorry he has lost an eye in the cause. His cheeriness, however, illustrates the remarkable good spirits which prevail at the Front.

It is good to hear that Lionel Appleyard and Alfred Sykes, who were wounded, are doing well. You will be sorry to know that Second Lieutenant George Hebblethwaite, reported missing, has not been heard of.   He had only recently been sent to join a new Battalion of his regiment.

Pte. H. Whitehead, 27181
Report from 21st November 1916:

Informant states that on July 3rd or 4th, at night at Contalmaison, 2nd Lieut Hebblethwaite was with a bombing party. He was hit in the eye by a piece of shrapnel and left the trench and walked towards the dressing station.

L/Cpl F. Beard, 5038
15 January 1917:

Informant states that between the 7th and 14th July 1916 in front of Contalmaison, we made the attack at midnight, we had only got about 50 yards when I saw Mr. Hebblethwaite killed. He was hit through the head by machine gun fire. He was just in front of me when the casualty happened. Two men turned him over, and said he was dead. We gained our objective, but retired about 4 o'clock the same morning. The ground where he fell was under a very heavy shell fire. He was my Platoon officer.

Cpl E Chadwick, 5074
30 July 1916:

Lt. Hebblethwaite was in B Coy. He was badly wounded in the abdomen on July 6th to the left of Contalmaison. I saw two stretcher bearers of the Duke of Wellington's Regt in a shell hole bandaging his wound. I was with the M/G Section. We were driven back at this point at dawn on the 8th by a German counter attack. I saw Mr. Hebblethwaite as we came back. I was almost the last man to come in. There would not be more than a dozen men behind me. The Germans came across the ground where Mr. Hebblethwaite lay. He could have been taken prisoner and if he did not die he probably was. He could not have got into our lines at this point.

Written extracts from service records
Men from George's Battalion were interviewed to try and confirm what happened to on the 7 July. The three reports taken during the investigation demonstrate the confusion that could arise during battle – perhaps influenced by the fact that George had only been with the Battalion for less than a month and that the attack had been undertaken in darkness. National Archive; George Hebblethwaite Service Records.[50]

James Blue with friends

Photograph of James Blue (seated, with a pipe) and three friends taken during training with the Honourable Artillery Company. The 'Arf a Mo' Kaiser! caption is a reference to a popular cartoon from 1914 of a British solider pausing to light a pipe. Courtesy of The University of Manchester.

Graves

The grave of William Leslie Wood (near left) at Essex Farm Cemetery near Ypres, Belgium. Essex Farm was a dressing station near the front line between April 1915 and August 1917. This cemetery is famous for the being the location that the poem 'In Flanders Fields' was written in 1915 by John McCrae of the Canadian Army Medical Corps. Author's own collection.

Second Lieutenant
HARRY THORNTON PICKLES

West Riding Regiment

Hulme Hall Resident No. 269
Killed in Action 1916

Born	11 March 1890
Date Entered Hulme Hall	October 1907
Degree Course	History
Regiment	9th West Riding Regiment
Killed in Action	26 April 1916, Armentières
Age	26
Buried	Cite Bonjean Military Cemetery, Armentières, France

Pre-War

Harry Thornton Pickles was born in 1890 in Barnoldswick, Yorkshire. Having completed his secondary education at Silcoates School in Wakefield, Harry accepted a place at the university to study History. Resident at Hulme Hall between October 1907 and June 1910, Harry was an influential and popular member of the Halls, spending his last year in the role of Senior Man. A keen footballer, Harry was considered a man of great character and persistency, extraordinarily efficient in everything he undertook, showing good judgement and real skill in adapting means to ends.

Graduating with a BA in 1910 with First Class honours in modern history, Harry completed an MA the following year. He joined a firm of solicitors in Manchester and began studying law, graduating in 1913 with honours. Going on to continue his law studies in London, he passed his solicitor's exams in 1914 with distinction, winning the Clements Inn and Daniel Rearden prizes. At the outbreak of war, Harry had been elected as a lecturer in English Law at the University of Manchester.

War Service

Harry initially enlisted in the 10th Battalion Duke of Wellington's West Riding Regiment at the outbreak of war. Having completed training he was commissioned as a Second Lieutenant, transferring to the 3rd Battalion in North Shields where he was responsible for training and organising troops before they left for overseas service. Harry himself was finally drafted to France in January 1916, marrying Ada Herf in Kent a week before he left.

On arrival, he was posted to the 9th Battalion. On his way to a grenade course in February he bumped into fellow Hulme Hall and History student, William Wildblood, in Poperinge. William wrote of the meeting to their tutor, Professor Tout, saying:[31]

> I met him quite by accident in old 'Pop' and took him to our mess for lunch. He was rather boyishly excited over his new experiences and I spent a very pleasant hour or two with him before he had to go.

In late April whilst in the front lines near Armentières, the Battalion became aware of the Germans preparing for an assault. For several days the German guns seemed to be rehearsing a range of tactical barrages on the British front line and communication trenches, heightening concerns of a forthcoming attack. The morning and afternoon of 26 April was quiet although from 5pm onwards the front line was relentlessly bombarded again which left the trenches in ruins. At 8pm German infantry launched an attack. Despite no man's land being covered in a thick smoke, the Battalion's Lewis guns opened fire into the gloom and managed to slow the attack. A number of enemy troops reached the shattered trenches but were swiftly thrown back. During the bombardment that day, Harry left the shelter of his dugout to check that the men under his command were safe. Having made his way through the trenches, he was caught by the blast of a shell as he leaned back on the parapet to talk to his men and was instantly killed by the concussion.

Having received notice of Harry's death, his parents later received a letter dated April 25, the day before he was killed, stating that he was feeling very fit.

'It was characteristic of Harry that he declined to seek a commission until he had thoroughly made himself conversant of the work of a soldier, and that it needed some persuasion to convince him that it was his duty to accept such preferment.' [32]

Lieutenant

WILLIAM ARTHUR WILDBLOOD

Army Service Corps

Hulme Hall Resident No. 282
Killed in Action 1917

Born	1 January 1889
Date Entered Hulme Hall	October 1908
Degree Course	History
Regiment	195th Company, Army Service Corps
Killed in Action	16 June 1917, Passchendaele
Age	28
Buried	Reninghelst New Military Cemetery, Belgium

Pre-War

William Arthur was born in Huddersfield on New Year's Day 1889 to the Rev Charles Bowers Wildblood and his wife Marion.

William completed his secondary education at Kingswood School in Bath where he enjoyed playing football and cricket. He entered Hulme Hall in October 1908 having been awarded a Hulme Hall scholarship to study History. He only stayed at Hulme Hall for a year, spending the final two years living with a friend.

Completing his degree in 1911, William took up an appointment as a teacher at Huddersfield Secondary School, leaving at the end of the 1913-1914 academic year. During his time at the school he played for Huddersfield Old Boys Rugby Union club. At the outbreak of war, he had taken up a place on the staff at Colston School in Bristol.

War Service

William joined the Bristol University OTC whilst applying, unsuccessfully, for a commission with the Royal Field Artillery (RFA) on several occasions. By Christmas 1914 he had grown frustrated at a lack of opportunity to join the RFA and took matters into his own hands. Leaving Colston School, he joined the House of Court Cavalry Squadron, a territorial unit responsible for training officers.

William trained with the Squadron for four months, embracing the long hours and hard, dirty work that looking after horses and stables entailed. William was able to develop his leadership skills, being appointed an NCO and becoming an important member of the Squadron staff. In May his hard work was rewarded when he received a commission in the Horse Transport and was sent to Aldershot for further training, passing the course with ease.

William was posted to 195th Company Army Service Corps (ASC) who were mobilised to France in late August 1915 as part of the 24th Divisional Train. William's role was transporting provisions and trench materials to troops on the front line. Writing to his former history tutor, Professor Tout, William noted that: [33]

Our work is behind the lines and not accompanied with the same risks as other units have to face. Our tours become very monotonous at times – an occasional shelling keeps us alive; but the high explosive shells are not a pleasant neighbour.

Despite sharing in the general hardships faced by fighting men, William was unfulfilled in his work. Having contributed during the Battle of the Loos, Ypres and the Somme, his unit were posted to a quiet part of the front by January 1917. Disappointed at what he perceived to be unimportant work in a 'cushy' part of the front, William applied again to the RFA. At first, his application was rejected due to the number of other ASC officers wanting to join the RFA. An agreement was struck that forty officers could transfer per month and by June 1917 William would have been delighted to receive news that his transfer request had been accepted.

Sadly, before he was able to complete the transfer William was killed by an enemy shell whilst supervising the unloading of supplies at Reninghelst Railway Station on the outskirts of Ypres.

'I am very sorry to have to tell you of the death of your son Will. We all feel his death very deeply: he was so very popular with all the officers and men.' Another officer says: 'We miss his happy smile very much, he being universally loved and respected by all his brother officers and men in the train and throughout the Division. There was about him a personal charm, a mingling of strength and grace, which won for him the affection of all.'[34]

Lieutenant

EYRE SPENSER WILKINSON

City of London (Royal Fusiliers)
Royal Flying Corps

Hulme Hall Resident No. 283
Killed in Action 1916

Born	31 July 1890
Date Entered Hulme Hall	October 1908
Resident Number	283
Course	Classical Studies
Regiment	1st Battalion City of London (Royal Fusiliers) & Royal Flying Corps
Killed in Action	12 January 1916, near Lens
Age	25
Buried	Chapelle D'Armentières New Military Cemetery, France

Pre-War

Eyre Spenser was born in 1890, the eldest son of Henry Spenser Wilkinson and his wife Victoria. Eyre attended Doon House School in Westgate-on-Sea and in 1904 entered Marlborough College as a scholar. In 1908 he continued his classical studies in Manchester whilst staying at Hulme Hall.

Eyre harboured ambitions to become an engineer; however, his doctors had discouraged a career in this field due to concerns around his health. On return from a tour in the Alps in 1909, his doctors pronounced him sound in all respects and he at once determined to prepare for the profession of his choice. Leaving Manchester and Hulme Hall, he went to Skinningrove Works at Saltburn and a year later enrolled at University College London and in 1911 at McGill University, Montreal.

The following summers were spent undertaking survey work for the Canadian Pacific Railway. In 1914 he was home for the summer in Chelsea when war broke out.

War Service

The very next day after war with Germany was declared, Eyre applied for a commission with the 1st Battalion City of London (Royal Fusiliers) Territorial Army Regiment. Accepted on 20 August 1914, Eyre was commissioned as a Second Lieutenant and in September was posted with the Battalion to Malta. After four months of intensive training, the Battalion were recalled to England and after a short period of leave arrived in Le Havre, France, in March 1915.

Eyre spent approximately eight months on the Western Front with his Battalion. During this time, he was involved in two major offensives: Aubers Ridge on 9 May and Bois Grenier on 25 September; a diversionary attack that formed part of the wider Battle of Loos.

Initially held in reserve for the Aubers Ridge attack, Eyre's Battalion suffered tremendous casualties when called upon to support a breakthrough by the 13th Battalion City of London Regiment. Upon leaving the trenches, the Battalion were instantly met by heavy rifle and machine gun fire and high explosive and shrapnel shells. Within minutes, over 120 men were killed or wounded.

By September, Eyre had been promoted to Lieutenant and was in charge of the Battalion's machine gun section. During the assault at Bois Grenier on

25 September, he was extremely fortunate to survive unscathed when caught in the blast of a high explosive shell, which destroyed his guns.

Although physically having come through these terrible experiences in the trenches, mentally the past eight months must have taken its toll. In October 1915, Eyre volunteered as an observer with the RFC, perhaps in an attempt to escape his torturous surroundings.

After a short period of training, Eyre was posted to 'C' Flight of No.1 Squadron RFC. The weather during the winter was treacherous – considered perfect flying conditions by many aircrew as it limited flying time!

On 12 January 1916 Eyre and his pilot, Second Lieutenant Robert Barton, were ordered to undertake a long reconnaissance patrol. They failed to return. Seventeen days later, a lone German aeroplane dropped a letter to the RFC confirming that both had been shot down and killed.

'The boy is gone, indeed, but I know something of the inner battles that he had to fight to which I think he won. He was with us five days in mid-December radiant and tender and I think with some presentiment of what was coming.' [35]

Major

HOWARD REDMAYNE HARKER, MC

Royal Flying Corps / Royal Air Force

Hulme Hall Resident No. 314
Died of Illness 1919

Born	12 May 1891
Date Entered Hulme Hall	October 1910
Degree Course	Engineering
Regiment	Royal Flying Corps / Royal Air Force
Decorations	Military Cross
Died of illness	27 February 1919
Age	27
Buried	Manchester Southern Cemetery, Manchester, England

Pre-War

Howard was born in 1891, the eldest of three children. His father, John Dent Harker, was a well-known architect in the north-west of England.

Howard attended Rossall School in Lancashire, distinguishing himself in sports where he played football and was captain of the hockey squad. Awarded a Hulme Hall Scholarship, Howard was resident at the Hall between 1910 and 1913 whilst completing an Engineering degree. He was active in Hall life, particularly in the inter-hall games against Dalton, in which he competed in football, cricket and swimming. In 1913 Howard was part of the Hulme Hall team who won the University Sports tug-of-war competition.

Leaving Manchester with a First Class Degree and the Fairburn Prize for Engineering, Howard started work in Farnborough with the Experimental Department at the Royal Aircraft Factory (RAF), a leading aircraft manufacturer at the time.

War Service

Whilst large numbers of men scrambled to serve their country, in 1914, Howard's applications were rejected time and time again, his work with the Royal Aircraft Factory being considered vital to the war effort. It wasn't until 1916 that Howard was finally accepted for training. The growing demand for pilots, combined with the fact he had become a talented pilot through his work went very much in his favour.

After completing training in May 1916, Howard joined the newly formed 57 Squadron in June, who flew aircraft that had been designed by the Royal Aircraft Factory. Having demonstrated both his knowledge of the aircraft he had helped to develop and his skills as a pilot, Harold was appointed as an instructor to new pilots joining the squadron. His quiet manner and cheerful disposition made him popular amongst his fellow officers.

In the winter of 1916, the Squadron were posted to France as a Fighter-Reconnaissance unit, starting operations in February 1917. Harold displayed a natural leadership and fought with great skill during fierce dog-fights against superior enemy aircraft time after time. In April, 57 Squadron lost eighteen aircrew (an entire squadron strength), either killed, wounded or taken prisoner. During this period, Harold was promoted to Captain and put in charge of 'A'

Flight. In June, the Squadron became a Bomber-Reconnaissance unit, their old aircraft being replaced.

In September 1917, after over ten months of the stress and strain of life as a front-line pilot, Harold was awarded the Military Cross and posted back to Britain to command a training squadron. During his time in France Howard had flown countless hours and missions, shot down at least five enemy aircraft. He had also fought against von Richthofen's 'flying circus' squadron; the one recorded dogfight occurred a day after the Red Baron had left for a period of leave back in Germany. During the fight, Harker's observer, Lieutenant Van Dyke Fernald, shot down an enemy plane, although the pilot made a successful landing.

On 27 February 1919, he succumbed to pneumonia brought on by influenza.

Military Cross Citation – London Gazette *9 January, 1918*

For conspicuous gallantry and devotion to duty. For nearly a year he has carried out extremely valuable work in taking aeroplane photographs and leading bombing raids far behind the enemy lines, often in the face of great opposition and trying weather conditions.

'On a recent occasion while returning from a successful bombing raid his formation was attacked by more than twice its number, but by his fine offensive spirit and skilful leadership, the enemy were dispersed. He has consistently set a splendid example to his brother officers.' [36]

Flight Lieutenant

CHARLES HAMILTON MURRAY CHAPMAN

Royal Navy Air Service

Hulme Hall Resident No. 315
Killed in an Aircraft Accident 1918

Born	24 March 1892
Date Entered Hulme Hall	October 1910
Degree Course	General, including Geology
Regiment	Royal Navy Air Service
Killed in Flying Accident	23 February 1918
Age	25
Buried	All Saints Church, Eastbourne, Isle of Sheppey

Pre-War

Charles Hamilton Murray Chapman was born in 1892 in Coleford, Gloucestershire.

Murray, as he was known, entered Hulme Hall in October 1910 having completed his secondary education at Monmouth Grammar School. His first year was spent completing a foundation course which included classes in geology in preparation for starting a degree in the subject.

He quickly gained a reputation at Hulme Hall for originality in thought and action and for his never-failing sense of humour. His keen interest in geology and astronomy proved to be a constant source of inspiration to him. He contributed articles to several scientific journals and wrote a book on pre-historic animals which he had hoped to publish.

However, Murray struggled academically and left Manchester at the end of his second year in 1912.

War Service

At the outbreak of war Murray volunteered with the Royal Navy and, with his knowledge of wireless telegraphy, was given a post as a wireless operator on board HMS *Revenge*. During his time at sea, he took part in action off the Belgium coast in October 1914.

In January 1915 he was transferred to a mine-sweeper where he spent the first winter of the war patrolling the North Sea. Even the monotony of this work couldn't dampen Murray's spirit, with reports that he still managed to derive much amusement from his time at sea.

In June, Murray received a commission in the Royal Naval Air Service (RNAS) and began training to be a pilot, receiving his licence at the end of July. Pilots received their licences from the Royal Aero Club of Great Britain at the time, and the photograph posed by Murray on qualifying appears to capture his character perfectly.

During his career as a pilot, he met with several accidents, the most serious occurring in France when he crash landed after suffering engine failure, a common problem with aeroplanes at the time, breaking his jaw. In his obituary in the Hulme Hall Chronicle it was noted that even these mishaps failed to dampen his enthusiasm and gave him the opportunity to write vivid and detailed accounts of the sensations experienced whilst crashing to earth.

It took six months to recover from the accident during which time Murray met and married Olive Simpson in March 1916.

Having been declared fit by the Navy, Murray was appointed as an instructor. He soon tired of this role and resumed full duties a short time later. On 23 February 1918, Murray was part of an escort flight assigned to protect an airship. Whilst over the Isle of Sheppey, he was involved in a mid-air collision with another aircraft which was to cost the lives of all four aircrew involved.

Having shared her husband's adventurous nature, Olive Chapman went on to become a famous explorer in the 1930s, publishing a number of books. Olive changed her middle name on her books from Mary to Murray in his honour.

Determined that her husband's memory would live on, Murray's wife, with support of his family, ensured that the book he had spent so much time writing and illustrating before the war went to press. Dragons at Home *was published in 1924. The book tells of a journey made by four children into the past, assisted by a pterodactyl.*

Lieutenant
ARTHUR MORTON GOODALL

Durban Light Infantry
South Africa Infantry

Hulme Hall Resident No. 317
Killed in Action 1916

Born	3 June 1892
Date Entered Hulme Hall	October 1910
Degree Course	Engineering
Regiment	Durban Light Infantry and 6th South African Infantry
Killed in Action	21 March 1916
Age	23
Buried	Moshi, Tanzania

Pre-War

Arthur Morton was born in Lower Bebington, Cheshire, in 1892 to Frederick and Emily Goodall.

The Goodall family moved to South Africa shortly afterwards and Arthur completed his secondary education at Bishop's College, Cape Town, passing matriculation at the Cape of Good Horn University before accepting a place at the Victoria University of Manchester to study Engineering.

Entering Hulme Hall in October 1910, Arthur enjoyed student life and took an active part in student affairs and was a popular member of the Men's Union. Playing rugby for the university, he was a regular in the Second XV and won Athletic Colours at Hulme Hall for his contribution to the tug-of-war and swimming teams. He was also a member of the OTC, attaining the rank of Lance Corporal.

Arthur did not pass the first two years of his degree and in July 1913 he left Manchester and returned to Durban, South Africa, where he had accepted an engineering position with Lever Brothers. In January 1914, Arthur applied for, and received, a commission with the Durban Light Infantry.

War Service

At the outbreak of war, the South African government declared their support for the Allies. This was despite internal opposition from many Afrikaans who were against fighting alongside the British so soon after the Second Boer War which had ended twelve years earlier.

Germany had colonised two large areas of Africa in the 1880s, creating German South-West Africa and German East Africa. After a failed attempt to invade German South-West Africa in 1914, the German's launched a pre-emptive attack on South Africa in February 1915.

Two battalions of the Durban Light Infantry were involved in the resulting invasion that followed on the heels of the defeat of the German and Afrikaans Army during the Battle of Kakamas. It hasn't been determined which Battalion Arthur fought with: the 1st Battalion were involved in fighting to the north of South-West Africa, whilst the 2nd Battalion were responsible for maintaining lines of communication.

After returning to South Africa following the successful defeat of the enemy by July 1915, Arthur and a large number of his comrades volunteered to continue fighting against the Germans in German East Africa, forming the core of the 6th African Infantry Regiment (AIR).

In March 1916 the British launched an attack through the Taveta Gap from British East Africa into German East Africa, capturing the nearby town of Moshi, near Mount Kilimanjaro. The 6th AIB formed part of the 2nd South African Infantry Brigade (SAIB) who followed in reserve.

On 21 March 1916, Lieutenant Arthur Goodall found himself attacking heavily defended German trenches along the line of the Soko River with the 2nd SAIB. Facing fierce resistance, the South African Infantry were forced back. During the attack, Arthur went to the aid of his Sergeant who had been badly wounded. Whilst bandaging the wounds, Arthur was hit and killed. Arthur is now buried in Moshi, Tanzania, in the foothills of Mount Kilimanjaro.

'Arthur possessed the gift of friendship in a marked degree, and was very popular in the Hall and at the University. He was a familiar figure, in cowboy costume, at the Shrove Tuesday celebrations, and entered into all University activities with enthusiasm. In him the Hall loses one of its stalwarts'. [37]

Captain

WILLIAM ORLANDO JONES

South Wales Borderers

Hulme Hall Resident No. 318
Killed in Action 1917

Born	28 December 1892
Date Entered Hulme Hall	October 1910
Degree Course	Architecture
Regiment	10th Battalion, South Wales Borderers
Killed in Action	26 August 1917
Age	24
Buried	Bards Cottage Cemetery, Boezinge, Belgium

Pre-War

William Orlando Jones was born in 1892 in Pontypridd, where his father was proprietor of Pontwyn Merthyr Colliery.

William completed his secondary education at Porth County School, passing the Central Welsh Board Senior examinations in 1909. Moving to Manchester to study Architecture in 1910, he resided at Hulme Hall where he became a popular member of the community.

Completing his degree in July 1913 with First Class Honours, William was awarded a Travelling Scholarship in Architecture with which he went to Italy to study at the British School in Rome. On his return to England, the Glamorgan County Council awarded him a special scholarship for original work in architecture.

War Service

Such was the response to Lord Kitchener's appeal for volunteers in August 1914, the numbers of men wanting to join the army as officers far outweighed the openings available. Those who found themselves in this situation could either enlist as a solider with the hope of gaining a commission later or continue in their current employment and wait for a commission to be awarded.

William chose the former, enlisting with the newly formed University & Public Schools (UPS) Brigade in September 1914. As the war continued beyond the first couple of months, the demand for officers for Kitchener's New Army became apparent. Filled with men from public schools and universities, the UPS Brigade provided a significant number of men from its ranks to serve as officers in other Battalions. By April 1915, over 3000 men from the UPS had been awarded commissions; William was one of this number, receiving his commission in January 1915 with the 10th Battalion South Wales Borderers (SWB).

The 10th Battalion SWB were formed in October 1914 and were training in Colwyn Bay when William joined them. Displaying the same skill and talent as an officer as he did as a student, William was promoted to Lieutenant in mid-1915 and to Captain in December 1915, just prior to the Battalion landing in France having successfully completed their training.

Having spent six months operating in and out of the trenches as part of the 38th (Welsh) Division, the Battalion were involved in the taking of Mametz Wood in July 1916 during the Battle of the Somme. The Battalion suffered greatly, not returning to significant action again until the Third Battle of Ypres, often referred to as Passchendele, during which they were involved in the opening attacks of the offensive known as the Battle of Pilckem Ridge, 31 July–2 August 1917.

William by this time was commanding B Company, who, combined with the rest of the Battalion, suffered almost 200 casualties during the three-day battle, which took place in torturously wet conditions. After a brief period of rest and training to regroup, the Battalion returned to the front lines near Langemarck on 18 August.

The Battalion war diaries note that before and after midnight of 25/26 August, B Company Headquarters were shelled with gas shells and suffered considerably.

William was caught up in the gas attack, dying shortly afterwards. He was buried nearby in Bards Cottage Cemetery, located only six miles away from his younger brother, Trevor Anwyl, who had been killed two months previously whilst serving with the 72nd Field Ambulance.

'Lieutenant Colonel Harvey wrote concerning him [William]: "He was a gallant officer, full of spirit, determination and grit, and always cheerful. He has done some really good work out here. I have lost a good and reliable officer."' [38]

Lieutenant

AUBREY HARRIS

Manchester Regiment

Hulme Hall Resident No. 331
Killed in Action 1916

Born	13 October 1893
Date Entered Hulme Hall	October 1911
Degree Course	French
Regiment	21st Battalion, Manchester Regiment
Killed in Action	4 September 1916
Age	22
Commemorated	Thiepval Memorial, Albert, France

Pre-War

Born in Wrexham in 1893, Aubrey attended Hawarden County School.

Having successfully completed his examinations with the Central Welsh Board in 1909, he entered Hulme Hall in October 1911 to study French at the university.

Popular amongst his fellow students, Aubrey was an accomplished sportsman, excelling particularly at rugby where he played regularly for the University 1st XV.

Aubrey successfully graduated in the summer of 1914 and secured a teaching post at Merchiston Lodge School in Edinburgh where he became involved with the OTC.

War Service

Aubrey left Merchiston Lodge School with ten other teachers in December 1914 to join the 21st Battalion of the Manchester Regiment. The 21st Battalion were one of the Manchester Pals Battalions.

Aubrey moved with the Battalion to Morecambe to start training in January 1915. In April of the same year, the Battalion moved to Grantham and Aubrey was promoted to Lieutenant and put in charge of the Battalion bombers. Bombers were infantry who were trained in the art of grenade throwing; critical for either attacking enemy trenches or defending your own.

In September the Battalion moved again, this time to Salisbury Plain where they undertook their final stages of training before proceeding to France in November 1915 to join the 7th Division. Even having arrived in France, the Battalion continued to train, waiting for several months before being assigned to a front-line posting on the Somme, near the village of Mametz, in February 1916.

For five months Aubrey and his Battalion rotated in and out of the front line opposite Mametz. Whilst on 'rest days' the Battalion were often put to work on the new narrow gauge railways being prepared for the major assault planned for the summer.

Held in reserve during the initial, now infamous, attack on the 1 July, Aubrey and his men waited in nervous anticipation having built up to the attack for months.

The Battalion didn't have to wait long, soon being called upon to support the attack of their colleagues in the 7th Division from the 2nd Battalion Queens (Royal West Surrey) and 22nd Manchester Battalion on Mametz. Despite suffering heavy casualties, the division captured the targets set for them.

In the following weeks the 21st Battalion continued to support attacks across the region. In late July, Aubrey fought at High Wood with the Battalion; again suffering heavy casualties.

On 4 September, the bombers of the 21st Battalion were used in an attack out from Delville Wood against enemy trenches near Ginchy.

Aubrey wasn't scheduled to take part, but he was killed when going forward to investigate how the assault was progressing, becoming one of the 227 casualties suffered by the Battalion during the failed attack.

'My very best pal, your son Aubrey, was killed with a shell on the evening of the fourth of September. We had come forward together to find Captain Cunliffe and his Company to discover what the situation was like.

I left them together and returned to the Brigade with what news we had gathered. He remained behind doing more than his duty in keeping Captain Cunliffe company. Two hours later some of his men came back and reported to me that both he and Captain Cunliffe had been killed instantaneously by the same shell. The news quite broke me – I pray you may be able to bear it.' [39]

Captain

ROBERT HAROLD BEDFORD

Manchester Regiment

Hulme Hall Resident No. 333
Killed in Action 1918

Born	11 August 1892
Date Entered Hulme Hall	October 1911
Degree Course	History
Regiment	6th Battalion, Manchester Regiment
Decorations	Mentioned in Dispatches
Killed in Action	25 March 1918
Age	25
Commemorated	Pozières Memorial, Pozières, France

Pre-War

Robert Harold Bedford was born in 1892 in Openshaw, Manchester.

He attended Manchester Municipal Secondary School where he developed a keen interest in History.

Obtaining the Jones History Scholarship, Robert arrived at Hulme Hall in October 1911 to commence a degree in History at the university. He was an active member of Hulme Hall, the Historical Society and the University OTC.

Robert graduated in 1914 and is believed to have been at the OTC Summer Camp in August when news that Britain had declared war with Germany broke.

War Service

Robert volunteered for active service on the OTC's return to Manchester after the Summer Camp. He was commissioned in September 1914 as Second Lieutenant in the 6th Battalion Manchester Regiment. After training with the reserve Battalion, he was drafted to the Dardanelles in July 1915, arriving in Gallipoli to take part in the unsuccessful attacks in August. Robert survived the terrible conditions at Gallipoli, noting in letters to his History tutor, Professor Tout: [40]

> The smells in those same trenches are truly appalling and the spectacle of lines of unburied corpses in front – many of them one's own chums; does not add any enjoyment to the condition of things. It was the dreadful frontal assaults that laid our men in heaps. In the trenches one stands a reasonable chance of survival but once over the parapet you are in the roll of honour.

After being evacuated from Gallipoli, Robert and the 6th Battalion were posted to Egypt. By this time Robert had been promoted to Captain but despite leaving the hardships of Gallipoli he found life in Egypt dull and was grew frustrated at the lack of opportunity to fight: [40]

> The inactivity here is worse than the trenches in the thick of the fighting…
> to read of the furious fighting on every front save the Egyptian makes one feel an outsider and a slacker.

Robert received his wish in February 1917 when the Battalion arrived on the Western Front. The remainder of the year was eventful; Robert was involved in advances in April when the German Army pulled back to their Hindenburg Line. He was also wounded twice: firstly, in September he was caught in a shell blast and at the same time gassed, becoming temporarily blind for almost four days. In November, he was struck in the foot by shrapnel.

In March 1918, during the early stages of the Ludendorff Offensive, the last-ditch German effort to win the war, Robert intercepted a messenger who was going to headquarters to request assistance. Gathering a number of men from his company he advanced to provide support but ran into a nest of machine guns in Bibicourt Wood, on the Somme, where it is presumed the whole party was wiped out.

'I have it in command from His Majesty the King to inform you, as next-of-kin of the late Captain Robert Bedford of the Manchester Regiment (Territorial Force) that this Officer was mentioned in a Despatch from Field Marshal Sir Douglas Haig dated 7th April, 1918 and published in the seventh Supplement to the London Gazette *of 21st dated 24th May, 1918, for gallant and distinguished service in the Field.*

I am to express to you the King's high appreciation of their service and to add that His Majesty trusts that their public acknowledgement may be of some consolation in your bereavement.' [41]

Private

STEPHEN AMBROSE FISHER

Royal Fusiliers

Hulme Hall Resident No. 350
Killed in Action 1916

Born	13 August 1891
Date Entered Hulme Hall	January 1912
Degree Course	Engineering
Regiment	20th Battalion Royal Fusiliers
Killed in Action	23 July 1916
Age	24
Buried	St Sever Cemetery, Rouen, France

Pre-War

Stephen Ambrose Fisher was born in 1891 in Windermere where his father was an Inspector of Schools in the Lake District.

Following his father's death, Stephen attended Blundell's School in Tiverton, Devon. Keen to become an engineer, he spent a year at the Hill's Works at Sheffield before being accepted onto the Engineering course at Victoria University of Manchester. Stephen joined Hulme Hall mid-way through the year in January 1912.

Stephen was known to have an unassuming, friendly nature that endeared him to his fellow students at Hulme Hall. He spent the summer vacations stoking on tramp ships and liners going to and from America.

A keen rugby player, Stephen had broken into the University Rugby 1st XV by the 1913/14 season. He also played in a friendly against the Canadian National Team.

War Service

Stephen enlisted with the 3rd Public School Battalion (PSB) of the University & Public Schools (UPS) Brigade in Manchester in September 1914. The 3rd PSB were later attached to the Royal Fusiliers, becoming the 20th Battalion of the Regiment.

Stephen successfully completed basic training in the south-east of England and was assigned as a machine gunner. In a letter to the Rev T Nicklin after his death, Stephen's aunt wrote:[42]

> He joined the 20th Battalion of the Royal Fusiliers as a private and was very about soldiering, keeping his gun and accoutrements in excellent order. He used to work the machine gun of D Company and was very keen about it.

Stephen and the Battalion had to wait for over a year before they were considered ready to fight, being mobilised to the Western Front in November 1915.

Arriving in France on 14 November as part of 33rd Division, within a week the Battalion were moved to Béthune, near Lens, to work alongside Battalions of the Scottish Rifles and Argyle & Sutherland Highlanders, gaining experience operating on the front line. By December they were considered fully operational and ready to man trenches on their own.

For the next seven months Stephen and the Battalion settled down into a steady routine of rotating through the front-line, support and reserves trenches with other Battalions in their Division, as well as spending time in training and rest camps. Danger and death were always lurking however, and the war diaries record that casualties were suffered at a steady rate.

At the start of the Somme Offensive in July 1916, the Battalion were operating near Lens. With casualties being much higher and progress much slower than expected, the 33rd Division were brought in to provide support, arriving in the region on 10 July.

Ten days later, in the early hours of 20 July the Battalion took part in an unsuccessful attack on High Wood. Attempting to surprise the enemy by using a creeping barrage as cover, the Battalion were eventually exposed and cut down, suffering 386 casualties. Stephen was badly wounded during the attack, eventually being evacuated to No.1 Australian General Hospital near Rouen where he succumbed to his injuries and died three days later.

'After his death, Stephen's mother had such nice letters from his comrades talking of his straightforwardness, unselfishness and bravery. The Sergeant wrote for all the officers were killed.' [42]

Second Lieutenant

HARLAND WATTS

South Lancashire Regiment

Hulme Hall Resident No. 358
Died of Wounds 1916

Born	3 June 1894
Date Entered Hulme Hall	October 1912
Degree Course	History
Regiment	7th Battalion South Lancashire Regiment
Died of Wounds	22 November 1916
Age	22
Buried	Contay Military Cemetery, Contay, Somme, France

Pre-War

Born in 1894 in Thurlstone, Penistone, Harland attended Penistone Grammar School.

In October 1912 Harland began a degree studying History, having been awarded both Hulme Hall and University Scholarships.

As with many of his contemporaries, he joined the University OTC in October 1913 and would have been attending the summer camp in August 1914 when war was declared.

War Service

Harland appears to be unique amongst his Hulme Hall contemporaries. Despite his involvement with the OTC, he did not appear to get caught up in the excitement and rush to seek a commission or enlist with the army in 1914, choosing instead to complete his degree before being commissioned in June 1915 into the 10th Battalion South Lancashire Regiment. The 10th Battalion were a training Battalion, responsible for preparing men for service with other South Lancashire Battalions.

Harland proved to be a natural platoon instructor, responsible for around 100 men at a time although he often found himself in charge of a whole company, which would consist on average of 400 recruits. In mid-1916 Harland successfully completed a three-week musketry course, obtaining a First Class musketry instructor's certificate. As a result, he had additional responsibilities in running the regiment musketry courses for officers and NCOs.

In between training recruits and teaching musketry, Harland married Sarah Johnson on 24 April 1916 at his local parish church in Thurlstone.

Despite his work and home life keeping him busy, Harland was expecting to be released from training to service overseas. Writing to Professor Tout, his former History tutor, in June 1916, he said:[43]

> I don't know how long I shall be here but I should have been out at the front long ago, had it not been for the lack of a qualified musketry officer to take my place in the Battalion.

He added that his time instructing would soon come to an end:[43]

> I formed a platoon and had this time two officers' supernumerary attached to me. These people I trained fully and they are now standing by expecting a draft of officers shortly from one of the Cadet Battalions, so that may release some of us for service overseas.

Harland's thoughts proved to be true, and by the end of August he had been posted to the 7th Battalion South Lancashire Regiment. The Battalion had suffered heavy casualties, particularly amongst their officers, during the first seven weeks of the Somme offensive, with Harland being one of thirteen replacement officers.

On 18 November, in appalling conditions, Harland and the Battalion were involved in an attack on the village of Grandcourt, on what would turn out to be the official last day of the Battle of the Somme. The circumstances of Harland's wounding were reported to his family in a letter from his Commanding Officer:

> He was leading a Carrying Party up to a position, just taken under heavy fire in a most gallant manner, when he was wounded.

Harland was evacuated to the 49th Casualty Clearing Station where he died as a result of his wounds four days later. It was reported in the Hulme Hall Chronicle that Harland's death hit those still at the Hall hard, where he had many close friends.

'During this time, [Harland's platoon] were inspected by the Brigadier General, who complimented me very highly on my men and suggested to my CO that he should keep an eye on me for promotion – but I'm afraid the Colonel is rather impervious to such hints, seeing that this is the second time I've been recommended and nothing has come of it.' [43]

Second Lieutenant

JAMES GRIEG MITCHELL HENDERSON, MC

Rifle Brigade

Hulme Hall Resident No. 360
Killed in Action 1916

Born	19 August 1894
Date Entered Hulme Hall	October 1912
Degree Course	Science
Regiment	5th Battalion Rifle Brigade attached 3rd Battalion and 4th Battalion
Awards	Military Cross, Mentioned in Dispatches
Killed in Action	18 August 1916
Age	21
Buried	Delville Wood Cemetery, Longueval, France

Pre-War

James was born in India in 1894 where his father, the Rev James Henderson, served with the Church of Scotland in Bombay. Educated at Portsmouth Grammar School, James had ambitions to work with the Indian Forest Service.

He entered Hulme Hall in October 1912 having been awarded a place at the university to study for a Science degree. Another keen sportsman, Henderson represented Hulme Hall in the inter-hall matches in swimming and tug-of-war. During the 1913/14 season he was a regular member of the University 2nd XV rugby team and made several appearances for the 1st XV.

A member of the University OTC, Henderson was attending the annual summer camp when war broke out.

War Service

The death of his friend, and fellow Hulme Hall resident, Wilfred Trevelyan on 4 May 1915 near Ypres would have hit James hard. James and Wilfred had joined the 5th Battalion Rifle Brigade at the same time and had both been posted overseas to the 4th Battalion only a few weeks before Wilfred's death.

On 8 May, only four days after Wilfred was killed, James escaped a similar fate when defending his position against an enemy onslaught. In an engagement that was later to be known as the Battle of Frezenberg, James and sixty of his men fought alongside soldiers of the Princess Patricia's Canadian Light Infantry, holding back at least three separate waves of German attacks. Only four of his men were able to march out of the trenches with James at the end of the engagement. It was for his actions on this day that he was to be later awarded the Military Cross.[44]

The following month James spent a week in hospital having contracted German Measles and in August he was wounded for the first time when struck by a ricochet bullet in his left hip whilst in front-line trenches near Bois Grenier.

Upon recovery, James was posted to the 3rd Battalion in November 1915. Only two months later, in January 1916, he was wounded for a second time whilst operating in the front-line trenches, this time being hit in the face by a shell fragment. In the same month, James would learn that he had been awarded the Military Cross and mentioned in Sir John French's Dispatches.

SECOND LIEUTENANT JAMES GRIEG MITCHELL HENDERSON, MC

It took a further four months for James to recover significantly enough to be considered fit for active service. During his rehabilitation he spent several days at Hulme Hall and also wrote to the War Office to enquire whether he was entitled to a gratuity payment for his injuries. His claim was rejected as the wounds were not considered to cause permanent disfigurement.

In June 1916, James rejoined the 3rd Battalion as they prepared for the Somme Offensive. In July, he would have received news that he had been awarded a degree in absentia.

On 18 August, the Battalion were involved in an attack on the village of Guillemont, during which James was killed. He was buried the next day by his colleagues, on what should have been his 22nd birthday.

James distinguished himself greatly during the attacks of 18 August, capturing a German machine gun single-handed, and taking its Officer prisoner. His Colonel wrote afterwards that had Henderson lived, he would have sent his name to HQ for further honours. [45]

Second Lieutenant

WILFRED TREVELYAN

Rifle Brigade

Hulme Hall Resident No. 361
Died of Wounds 1915

Born	10 October 1893
Date Entered Hulme Hall	October 1912
Degree Course	Coal Mining
Regiment	5th Battalion Rifle Brigade attached 4th Battalion Rifle Brigade
Died of wounds	4 May 1915
Age	21
Commemorated	Menin Gate, Ypres, Belgium

Pre-War

The second son of Sir Ernest Trevelyan, Wilfred was born in Calcutta, India, in 1893 where his father was a High Court Judge. Moving back to England in 1900, Wilfred was educated at Rugby School where he was a member of the school OTC.

Although passing the entrance exam to Balliol College in Oxford, Wilfred was offered employment in India subject to obtaining a degree in coal mining. Agreeing to this, he arrived at Hulme Hall in October 1912 to study at the university. Wilfred was a popular figure at Hall and the university. By 1914 he was a regular in the 1st XV rugby team and was a successful boxer, receiving university colours in both sports. Wilfred was also a keen swimmer and cricketer, playing for Hulme Hall in inter-hall events.

War Service

Having joined Hulme Hall on the same day, both played for the University 1st XV Rugby team and served in the University OTC together, it was no surprise that Wilfred and James Henderson both applied and received temporary commissions into the 5th Battalion The Rifle Brigade at the same time in August 1914. Having both been born in India, The Rifles were a natural regiment of choice given their history of service in Asia.

In March 1915, Wilfred and James were posted to France and attached to the 4th Battalion, entering the war at a time where the life expectancy of a Second Lieutenant was six weeks.

Wilfred spent his first nine days in Belgium familiarising himself with the responsibilities of an infantry officer, taking his place on the front line for the first time in early April near Ypres.

April also marked the start of a series of battles known as the Second Battle of Ypres, where the German Army tried to break through the Allied trenches around the historic Belgium market town. This battle has become infamous as it was the first time that gas was used on the Western Front. Whilst not directly facing German attacks, the 4th Battalion were moved around to act as support in the event of an enemy breakthrough.

The month of April had been a baptism of fire for Wilfred and James. Within thirty days they had spent eighteen either on the front line or in reserve trenches, marched through Ypres as it was being shelled, been subject to gas attacks and seen tremendous losses to fellow Battalions. Two officers and thirty-two men were killed from their own Battalion, with over ninety being wounded.

On the 3rd May, the Battalion were moved to the eastern edge of Bellewaerde Wood close to Hodge Chateau, where they were ordered to dig a second line of trenches in Sanctuary Wood. During a German bombardment of the trenches the next day, tragedy struck. The incident was described by Captain de Moleyns in a letter to Wilfred's father.

'On Tuesday we had breakfast together, and shortly after that I took him up and asked him to get his men on to work at improving a communication trench. This trench was some way behind the actual fire trenches, and there had only been intermittent shell fire on it previously. I had only left Wilfred there a few minutes when the Company Sergeant-Major told me your son had been hit by a shrapnel shell. I went back at once and assisted him to the dressing station. He was very brave and cheery, and could walk with little or no support, and only complained of the pain in his back, where he had been hit, and giddiness. It was only early on yesterday morning that I heard he had died early in the morning.' [46]

Lieutenant

ALFRED EDWARD HOLTON, MC

Royal Marines Artillery

Hulme Hall Resident No. 362
Died of Illness 1919

Born	5 August 1890
Date Entered Hulme Hall	October 1912
Degree Course	Engineering
Regiment	Royal Marines Artillery
Awards	Military Cross
Died of Illness	22 February 1919
Age	28
Commemorated	Terlincthun British Cemetery, Boulogne, France

Pre-War

Alfred Edward Holton was born in Boudja, Smyrna (part of the Ottoman Empire) in 1890 where his father was working on the Aidin Railway. He and his brothers were educated privately in Boudja in a school set up by his mother.[47]

Alfred started work on the Aidin Railway once he had completed his secondary education. Keen to become an engineer, he applied for a place to study engineering at Victoria University of Manchester. He was accepted and entered Hulme Hall in October 1912.

No information has been located regarding Alfred's time at Hulme Hall, although it is known than he returned to Smyrna in the summers of 1913 and 1914 to continue working as an engineer on the ever-expanding railways.

War Service

Exactly what happened to Alfred between August 1914 and November 1915 is unclear, although notes made under Alfred's name in the Hulme Hall Admissions Book provide an insight.

Alfred travelled back to Britain in the autumn of 1914. Under normal circumstances, he would have been travelling back to Manchester to complete his third year of his engineering degree. However, it is known that the first group of volunteers from Smyrna also came to England for training at the same time.

In April 1915, Alfred was involved in the Gallipoli landings, but very little is known of his involvement or exactly how he got there. Hulme Hall records confirm he was with the Australian forces in the Dardanelles before being assigned to the Royal Navy Division. Having grown up in the Ottoman Empire, being able to speak the local language and understand the culture, it is likely that Alfred found himself in some form of liaison role.

Living conditions at Gallipoli were dire, particularly as it was difficult to bury the bodies of those killed during fighting. As a result, disease was rife with the Allied records showing that over 50% of the 245,000 casualties sustained during the conflict were the result of illness. Alfred was one of those numbers having contracted dysentery at the end of September 1915. He was evacuated back to England where he recovered at a Royal Navy Hospital in Gosport.

In November Alfred was given a commission with the Royal Navy Marines and in March 1916 was posted to the Royal Marine Artillery training base at Eastney Barracks, in Portsmouth.

Having completed training, Alfred was posted to No.3 Howitzer Battery who were fighting in France. Alfred survived over two years of life as an Artillery Officer on the Western Front and was awarded the Military Cross. In February 1919 Alfred was still on active service in France where he contracted influenza and died as a result of complications arising from the illness.

Military Cross Citation – London Gazette 11 January 1919

For conspicuous and devotion to duty. On two consecutive nights he brought his gun into action under heavy fire. During the operations he has worked ceaselessly co-operating in four mounts and dismounts of a 15-inch howitzer, guiding it over shell-pitted roads with old and inadequate transport. He has in addition kept the battery unusually well supplied with ammunition. His management and keenness have helped to keep the gun in close touch with the advance. [48]

Captain

ALLAN HIGSON SMITH, MC

Lincolnshire Regiment
Royal Flying Corps / Royal Air Force

Hulme Hall Resident No. 364
Killed in Action 1917

Born	21 June 1892
Date Entered Hulme Hall	October 1912
Degree Course	Engineering
Regiment	10th Battalion Lincolnshire Regiment / Royal Flying Corps and Royal Air Force
Decorations	Military Cross
Killed in Action	21 August 1917
Age	24
Commemorated	Arras Flying Services Memorial, Arras, France

Pre-War

Born in 1892 in Grimsby, Allan was educated at Rydal Mount School in Colwyn Bay.

After leaving school, Allan moved to Lincoln where he took up a position with Engineering Company Messrs Foster and Co. After working for four years he took and passed the entrance examination at Victoria University of Manchester in September 1912, commencing a degree in Engineering in October. During the course of his studies, Allan lived at Hulme Hall.

Allan joined the OTC in October 1913 and was at the annual camp in August 1914 when war was declared.

War Service

Allan at once offered his services to the army; however, by October he still hadn't heard anything back from the War Office.

Taking matters into his own hands he approached the Grimsby Battalion of the Lincolnshire Regiment, being commissioned as a Second Lieutenant in November.

In early 1915 the army recognised that airpower would play a vital role in the war. As part of a recruitment drive, regiments were asked to nominate officers and men with engineering experience for training with the Royal Flying Corps. With six years of experience, Allan was identified and his name was put forward in March. Four months later he reported at Castle Bromwich to begin training as a pilot, successfully qualifying a month later in August.

By late 1915, Allan had been posted to 4 Squadron who were already fighting on the Western Front having been mobilised to France at the outbreak of hostilities.

The Squadron was responsible for a variety of roles including reconnaissance, photography, spotting or guiding artillery fire and, on occasions, dropping spies behind enemy lines.

Allan proved to be both a talented and tenacious pilot who fought for over ten months with the Squadron, during which time he was promoted to the rank of Captain, appointed Flight Commander and awarded the Military Cross. On 1 July 1916 the Squadron were assigned to support the Allied attacks on the Somme.

In September, having completed a tour of duty, Allan was transferred out of the front line for a period of rest, being appointed Commander Officer of an aerial gunnery school in France. In December, he slipped from an aeroplane fracturing his arm. The injury took three months to heal and left Allan with a permanent shortening of the left arm.

On return to duty he spent time with 53 Reserve Squadron and 63 Flight School before being posted to 21 Squadron on 15 August 1917. Only a few days later, Allan failed to return after a mission over enemy lines, his aeroplane being brought down by gunfire.

Military Cross Citation – London Gazette 25 August 1916

For most gallant and skilful work in connection with artillery. In one instance flying at 1,000 feet, under heavy fire, his information led to the destruction of two enemy batteries. On another occasion he flew under clouds for two hours at 600 feet, sending down information. His machine was repeatedly hit. He has set a fine example. [49]

Second Lieutenant

GEORGE HEBBLETHWAITE

Lancashire Fusiliers

Hulme Hall Resident No. 369
Killed in Action 1916

Born	26 April 1894
Date Entered Hulme Hall	October 1912
Degree Course	Arts
Regiment	10th Battalion Lancashire Fusiliers
Killed in Action	7 July 1916
Age	22
Commemorated	Thiepval Memorial, Albert, France

Pre-War

Born in Mirfield, Yorkshire, George was the third child of six born to Abraham and Harriot Hebblethwaite. Abraham was a farmer, his farm having been in the family for over 200 years.

George attended Mirfield Grammar School where he excelled academically, completing his studies in 1911. In October 1912, George moved to Hulme Hall whilst studying for an Arts Degree at Victoria University of Manchester.

During his time at Hulme Hall, George was a member of the OTC and he would have been at the annual OTC summer camp at the outbreak of war in August 1914.

War Service

In early September 1914, George and his younger brother Benjamin travelled from Mirfield to Halifax to volunteer to serve with the Duke of Wellington (West Riding) Regiment. Such was the number of men wanting to enlist, the brothers were told to come back several days later to start training.

With a new Battalion being formed from scratch there was a need to identify men suitable to hold positions as Non-Commissioned Officers (NCOs). Responding well to the demands of basic training, George was promoted to the rank of Lance Corporal in October 1914, Corporal two months later and Sergeant by March 1915.

In mid-August 1915 the Battalion received orders that they were to be mobilised to the Western Front, arriving in France five days later. Within a month, George and the Battalion were thrown into action for the first time near Bois Grenier, part of the Battle of Loos.

Two months later, George returned to England to begin an officer training course. After a gruelling eight months he was commissioned as a Second Lieutenant with the 13th Battalion Lancashire Fusiliers, returning to France on 13 June 1916. Upon arrival he was drafted into the 10th Battalion Lancashire Fusiliers who were preparing to take part in the offensive planned in the Somme region.

Held in reserve during the notorious attacks of 1 July, the 10th Battalion were ordered in the early hours of 5 July to capture Quadrangle Trench, near

Contalmaison. George and his colleagues successfully completed the task despite meeting stiff resistance. Two days later, the Battalion were ordered to take Quadrangle Support Trench. Shortly after midnight on 7 July, George led his men forward. Met immediately with heavy rifle and machine gun fire, they were forced back.

George was severely wounded and did not make it back to the British trenches being reported as Missing in Action. With no one certain as to his fate, his family were informed by telegram that:[50]

> G Hebblethwaite Lancashire Fusiliers reported missing July 7th. This does not necessarily mean that he has been killed.

With conflicting reports of his fate provided by men of his company, George's details were passed to the German Army via the USA Embassy in the hope that he had been taken prisoner. His family had to wait six weeks before being informed that George had been formally reported as killed in action on 7 July 1916. His body was never recovered and his name is remembered on the Theipval Memorial.

'Lt Hebblethwaite was in B Company. He was badly wounded in the abdomen on July 6th to the left of Contalmaison. I saw two stretcher bearers of the Duke of Wellington's Regt in a shell hole bandaging his wound. I was with the M/G Section. We were driven back at this point at dawn on the 8th by a German counter-attack. I saw Mr Hebblethwaite as we came back. I was almost the last man to come in. There would not have been more than a dozen men behind me. The Germans came across the ground where Mr Hebblethwaite lay. He could have been taken prisoner and if he did not die he probably was. He could not have got into our lines at this point.' [50]

Private

JAMES RICHARD BLUE

Honourable Artillery Company

Hulme Hall Resident No. 372
Killed in Action 1917

Born	12 September 1895
Date Entered Hulme Hall	October 1912
Course	Civil Engineering
Regiment	1st Battalion Honourable Artillery Company
Killed in Action	8 February 1917
Age	21
Commemorated	Thiepval Memorial, Albert, France

Pre-War

James was born in 1895 in Norwich, the only child of James Blue, a locomotive engineer, and his wife, Emma.

James' father died between 1901 and 1910 and census records show by 1911 his mother had found employment as a live-in housemaid to a Mrs Shorten.[51]

James attended Norwich Grammar School and in October 1912, having just turned seventeen, he moved to Hulme Hall to study for a certificate in Civil Engineering at the Victoria University of Manchester.

In early 1914, James left Manchester before completing his course having accepted a job with Messrs Dick Kerr & Co. who had been appointed as a contractor with the Metropolitan Water Board on a reservoir project in Staines.

War Service

In January 1916 the British government introduced conscription in response to a dwindling number of volunteers coming forward to join the Armed Forces. Prior to commencement of conscription, Lord Derby promoted a scheme whereby men could enlist and either join up straight away or sign up as a reserve with an obligation to fight if called upon at a later date.

James continued to work as an assistant draftsman on the reservoir project throughout 1914 and 1915. On 10 December 1915, five days before the proposed deadline for men to volunteer under Lord Derby's scheme, James enlisted, choosing to delay joining the army until his services were required. Returning to work, he was called up three months later on 18 March 1916, beginning training with the Honourable Artillery Company (HAC).

On 6 May, James transferred to the 3rd Battalion HAC who were based in Richmond Park. Five months later, in October, the Battalion were moved to billets in the Tower of London. On 18 November, James was posted to France with a draft of 101 men assigned as reinforcements for the HAC Regiment. Just over two weeks later, he was posted to D Company of the 1st Battalion HAC.

For the remainder of December 1916 and the majority of January 1917 the Battalion were involved in training exercises, drill, sports and general preparations for a return to action on the front line.

The weather conditions were poor throughout this period with persistent heavy rain and snow. To combat the onset of trench foot, the Battalion Medical Officer issued men with whale fat to rub into their feet. Regular foot inspections were also carried out. The weather took a toll on James, who was admitted sick to hospital on 13 December, returning to the Battalion two days later.

On 30 January, the whole Battalion were moved into front-line trenches near Beaumont-Hamel. Almost fourteen months after enlisting, James found himself face to face with the enemy.

On the evening of 7 February, the Battalion were part way through their second stint on the front line, in trenches near Grandcourt. Orders were received that they were to attack a nearby German stronghold at Baillescourt Farm. D Company were held in reserve whilst A and B launched the attack after a short artillery bombardment.

Although the attack was successful, the Battalion began to suffer casualties from German artillery. As D Company moved forward to provide support, James was hit by a shell fragment, dying from his wounds shortly afterwards.

'Prior to his death, James had been recommended for a commission with the Royal Engineers. In a letter to James' mother after he was killed, his platoon commander wrote, "I had a very high opinion of your boy both as a comrade and a friend."' [52]

Second Lieutenant
WILLIAM LAWTON

North Staffordshire Regiment

Hulme Hall Resident No. 379
Killed in Action 1916

Born	1 January 1896
Date Entered Hulme Hall	October 1912
Degree Course	Mathematics
Regiment	8th Battalion North Staffordshire Regiment
Killed in Action	3 July 1916
Age	20
Commemorated	Thiepval Memorial, Albert, France

Pre-War

Born in Hanley in Stoke-on-Trent in 1896, William attended Hanley Secondary School, where he shone academically.

Awarded both a Hulme Hall Scholarship and William Swifton Exhibition, William entered Hulme Hall in October 1913 having accepting a place at the university to study for an honours degree in Mathematics.

Although quiet and unassuming in manner, he was noted amongst his peers at Hulme Hall for his soundness and unswerving loyalty.

War Service

William was still eighteen years of age at the outbreak of the war and had just completed the first year of his degree. Not having joined the University OTC in his first year, William was quick to sign up on his return to Manchester in October 1914. Five months later he received a commission with the North Staffordshire Regiment, leaving for training in Oxford in February 1915. Finishing training in November 1915, William received orders to proceed to France to join the 8th Battalion North Staffordshire Regiment near Armentières.

For the next eight months, William rotated in and out of the front-line with the Battalion. As plans were mounted for the Allied offensive on the Somme in the summer of 1916, the Battalion were transferred to the area in preparation.

On the night of 30 June the Battalion moved up to the reserve lines at Tyler's Redoubt to the north of the village of Millencourt. Here they were issued rations and kit for the forthcoming attacks: an activity that didn't finish until 4.30am on the morning on 1 July. At 7.30am, over 20,000 men lost their lives going 'over the top' into a hail of bullets, shells and uncut wire.

Back at Tyler's Redoubt, William and his colleagues could not see or hear the murderous fire. At 8pm, they received orders to launch a night-time bombing attack on the village of La Boisselle. William and A Company were left behind as B, C and D company followed on the heels of the Battalion bombing unit. However, on their way up to the front, they found the communication trenches blocked with wounded men mainly from the Tyneside Scottish regiments who had been involved in the attacks in the morning. As a result, the bombing raid had to be postponed.

The Battalion were ordered to retry the attack the next evening. This time A Company, including William, were to be involved. Staff at Headquarters had agreed to ensure the communication trenches were clear but the Battalion encountered a number of wounded men on stretchers which again caused delays. The attack could not be postponed a second time: arriving at the front line at 4am, there was no time to brief the men on the plan of attack as dawn was approaching. The leading men from D Company launched the attack at 4.30am, with twenty-four separate bombing parties entering the village in front of the infantry troops. During the course of the attack, William was killed by a shell whilst leading his men forward.

'He was my Platoon Commander and a real gentleman too. I was with him up to the time when I got hit, and shells were bursting all around us and machine guns played upon us. He kept us together as if on parade. I don't think there was a cooler-headed man, nor a better leader in the British Army.'

He was hit by a shell near the village we captured from the Germans. He was ahead of his Platoon and was urging his men on when the shell hit them and I am sorry to say he was instantly killed. All the men in A Company are deeply sorry he has gone under and all who met him agree that there was not a better officer in the Regiment. I can tell you I have begun to miss him already as he was a good pal and all the men in the platoon regret his loss. Just before his death he was walking about the village (which was still held by the Germans) as if such things as bullets and shells did not existing [53].

'Your brother was a subaltern in the Company under my command and was killed in action on the morning of July 3 when we were storming La Boisselle. He was killed while leading his men in the village itself, being hit on the head. No one regrets his death more than I do myself as we can ill afford to lose such officers. May I offer on behalf of my Company our deepest sympathy at your great loss. Our casualties were heavy on that day but they were not in vain for we won and kept La Boisselle – one of the finest achievements of the big push.' [53]

Second Lieutenant
WILLIAM BIGHAM

Northumberland Fusiliers

Hulme Hall Resident No. 381
Died of Illness 1915

Born	4 March 1894
Date Entered Hulme Hall	October 1913
Degree Course	Chemistry
Regiment	13th Battalion Northumberland Fusiliers
Died of illness	6 September 1915
Age	21
Buried	Stoke-on-Trent (Hartshill) Cemetery, Stoke-on-Trent, England

Pre-War

William Bigham was born in 1894 in Stoke-on-Trent to William and Harriet Bigham, the eldest of six children.

As a boy he attended Hanley Secondary School. Having successfully passed the Oxford Senior Local Examination he remained at the school as an Assistant Master in the chemistry laboratory. He was also a Sunday School teacher at the local Presbyterian Church.

Having worked at Hanley Secondary School for two years, William decided to further his education and applied to study Chemistry at Victoria University of Manchester. Having been offered a place, he applied for, and won, a Hulme Hall scholarship, entering the Hall in October 1913.

William was passionate about research work and it was his ambition to return to this field once he had completed his degree.

During his time in Manchester he became a member of the University OTC. He was at the annual OTC summer camp at the outbreak of the war.

War Service

William applied for a commission into the army on the day of his return from the annual OTC Camp in August 1914 and whilst waiting for his application to be processed he returned to Hulme Hall to start the second year of his course. He received news in December that he had received a commission as a Second Lieutenant with the 13th Battalion of the Northumberland Fusiliers.

William began training shortly afterwards, joining the Battalion where they were based in Tring. By the time he arrived, the Battalion had moved from living under canvas in Halton Park, near Tring, into local billets across the county, returning back to canvas in May 1915. It wasn't until June that the Battalion first received rifles and they began training with them in earnest.

It was during this time that William developed an internal complaint. He visited the Battalion Medical Officer who referred him to a specialist. Although the issue was not considered serious, it was recommended that an operation be carried out to investigate further.

As the 13th Battalion prepared to mobilise to join the fighting on the Western Front in mid-September, William was admitted to University College

Hospital. The operation was a success, however the next day there were serious complications from which he did not recover.

'Enthusiastic and energetic in everything he took up, he will be greatly missed. An exceedingly promising scholastic career has been cut short by his death.' [54]

Captain

ROBERT GEORGE ALEXANDER DICKEY

Manchester Regiment
Royal Engineers

Hulme Hall Resident No. 385
Died of Wounds 1918

Born	20 February 1894
Date Entered Hulme Hall	October 1913
Degree Course	Chemistry
Regiment	5th Battalion Manchester Regiment/ Royal Engineers
Died of Wounds	14 November 1918
Age	24
Buried	St Michael's Church, Foulridge, Lancashire, England

Pre-War

Robert was born in February 1894, the eldest of two sons born to Dr Archibald Dickey and his wife, Marion. The family lived in Colne, Lancashire.

Robert received an early private education at Mostyn House, West Kirby and completed his secondary education at Ermysted's Grammar School. He excelled academically in his first year at Ermysted's and won the junior high jump competition. In his last year he was swimming champion and played for the 2nd XI cricket team. In 1909 Robert left Ermysted's to attend Sixth Form College at St Bees in the Lake District.

In October 1913, Robert entered Hulme Hall having been accepted to study Chemistry at the university. During his first year he continued to shine athletically, representing the university at rugby and gymnastics. He also joined the University OTC.

War Service

Robert was one of the many Hulme Hall men who applied for a commission when the OTC returned from their summer camp in August 1914. Three months later, Robert and fellow Hulme Hall student Harold Porter received commissions with the 2/5th Battalion Manchester Regiment, a second line Territorial Unit that would provide reinforcements to the 1/5th Battalion.

In July 1915, both Robert and Harold were posted to the 1/5th Battalion in Gallipoli as replacements following a failed attack on 4 June. They had only been in Gallipoli for a few weeks when they were involved in a diversionary attack on Turkish positions during an attempt to set up a new beachhead in Suvla Bay; both were wounded and evacuated to Egypt. Robert recovered from a wound to his thigh but Harold was to succumb to his injuries.

Robert was able to rejoin the Battalion in Gallipoli before they were evacuated to Egypt in December. The next year was spent in Sinai guarding the Suez Canal and included involvement in the Battle of Romani in August when enemy forces attempted to seize the canal.

In February 1917, the Battalion were posted to the Western Front. After a period of leave in November, Robert was attached to the Royal Engineers. By April 1918 he had been promoted to Captain and was working with the

1st Field Company who were divided into topographical, map, observation and sound-ranging sections.

In March 1918, the Germans launched a last-ditch offensive to win the war, which almost succeeded. After an attack on the Somme in March, the German Army started to prepare for another offensive in early April, this time in Flanders, with several days of bombardment preceding the attack. On 8 April, Robert was working in the small town of Mazingarbe, to the north-west of Lens, when he was seriously wounded in a gas attack.

The effects on Robert were horrendous as he suffered severe vomiting, conjunctivitis and laryngitis. Four days later he arrived at the 2nd Western General Hospital, Manchester. Although his health began to improve over the coming months, having been transferred to the Officers' Convalescent Hospital in Blackpool he died of pneumonia after contracting influenza.

Robert's brother, John Porter Yeates Dickey, entered Hulme Hall in October 1914. He served throughout the war with distinction, both with the 5th Battalion Manchester Regiment and the Royal Air Force as an Observation Officer. In 1919 he returned to continue his studies at Hulme Hall.

Second Lieutenant
HAROLD JAMES PORTER

Manchester Regiment

Hulme Hall Resident No. 386
Died of Wounds 1915

Born	8 May 1895
Date Entered Hulme Hall	October 1913
Degree Course	Medicine
Regiment	5th Battalion Manchester Regiment
Died of Wounds	15 August 1915
Age	20
Buried	Alexandria (Chatby) Military Cemetery, Egypt

Pre-War

Born in May 1895 to Jessie and Thomas Porter, Harold grew up in St Annes-on-Sea and attended King Edward VII School in Lytham between 1908 and 1913.

Following in his father's footsteps, he chose to study Medicine at the university. During his time in Manchester he resided at Hulme Hall, first arriving in October 1913.

Another keen member of the University OTC, Harold was also attending the annual summer camp when war broke out.

War Service

As with many other members of the OTC, Harold was quick to offer his service to the army at the outbreak of war, completing his application form for a commission into the 5th Battalion Manchester Regiment.

Whilst the application was processed, Harold continued with his studies at the university, finally leaving Hulme Hall in late November 1914 before receiving his commission on 10 December. With the 5th Battalion already serving overseas in Egypt, Harold joined the newly created 2/5th Reserve Battalion who were training in Southport and later in Crowborough, Sussex.

In April 1915, the Allied Armies launched the Gallipoli offensive. The Manchester Regiment were heavily involved in early action from May, with the 5th, 6th, 7th and 8th Battalions forming the Manchester Brigade within the 42 (East Lancashire) Division. On 4 June, all four Battalions were involved in an attack on the Turkish lines, which was to cost the lives of many of their number.

In response to the large number of casualties received, men from the reserve Battalions were drafted out to Gallipoli to help bring the front-line units back to strength. Having just completed five months of training, Harold was one of those called upon. Leaving England on 3 July, it took three weeks to meet up with their new colleagues in Gallipoli, arriving on 24 July.

By late July 1915 the Allies were preparing for another offensive in an effort to break the stalemate that had set in since the first landings and attacks earlier in the year. The plan called for an amphibious assault by British troops at Suvla Bay which would support a breakout by ANZAC troops.

The 42 Division were located further south on the Gallipoli peninsula and on 5 August they received orders that they were to launch a diversionary attack in order to prevent Turkish reinforcements being drawn northwards to Suvla Bay. The diversionary attack was later to be known as the Battle of Krithia Vineyard.

Whilst the Manchester Regiments did not attack until 7 August, men from the 5th Battalion, including Harold, were ordered to assist Infantry Battalions from 29 Division. Whilst leading his men in a charge across no man's land, Harold was severely wounded when struck by a bullet in the chest.

Taken back behind the British lines, it was six days before Harold could be evacuated from Gallipoli finally being admitted to 19 General Hospital in Alexandria, Egypt on 12 August. Unfortunately, Harold did not recover and succumbed to his wounds three days later.

At the time of Harold's death, his father, Thomas Porter, was a Captain serving as a Medical Officer with the Royal Field Artillery. [55]

Harold's cousin, Robert Nuttall Porter, who also studied Medicine at Manchester University, died in 1919 of an illness contracted on service with the Royal Army Medical Corps. [56]

Captain

ARTHUR LORD

Welsh Regiment

Hulme Hall Resident No. 386
Died of Wounds 1917

Born	6 June 1897
Date Entered Hulme Hall	October 1914
Degree Course	Medicine
Regiment	3rd Battalion Welsh Regiment, attached 1st, 14th and 15th Battalions
Died of Wounds	12 February 1917
Age	19
Buried	Mendinghem Military Cemetery, Belgium

Pre-War

Arthur was born in Colwyn Bay to Robert and Elizabeth Lord and educated at Clive House School, Old Colwyn and Haileybury College.

Whilst at Haileybury College Arthur was an active and enthusiastic member of the OTC where he attained the rank of Lance Corporal. Arthur won a Hulme Hall scholarship in early 1914 and he was preparing to start a degree in Medicine at Victoria Manchester University at the outbreak of the war.

War Service

On 6 June 1916, Arthur turned nineteen, the official age young men were eligible to serve overseas with the army. Arthur, however, was celebrating his 'unofficial' 21st birthday as a wounded veteran who had served for over four months on the Western Front. Recently prompted to the rank of Captain, he had been attached to the 14th Battalion Welsh Regiment and was preparing to return to France.

Arthur had presented himself to a recruitment office on Dickinson Street in Manchester in December 1914, at the age of seventeen, giving his correct date of birth. Although too young to serve overseas, he requested to join the 3rd Battalion Welsh Regiment, a newly formed training Battalion. It took two weeks for the appropriate paperwork to be completed, which included signatures from Arthur's father and the Hulme Hall Warden.

It isn't known whether it was a ruse or an oversight, but Arthur was transferred to the 1st Battalion in France in June 1915, having only just turned eighteen. Between July and September Arthur and the 1st Battalion were in the front line for a total of forty-one days.

On the evening of 1 October, the 1st Battalion were ordered to attack the formidable defensive trench network known as the Hohenzollern Redoubt, near Loos. Unable to conduct a reconnaissance due to arriving in the front-line trenches in darkness, the Battalion attacked but did not capture ground in front of a support trench that had been dug out towards the enemy previously to enable supplies and reinforcements to come up, effectively trapping themselves in the captured trenches. As dawn arrived and supplies, particularly bombs, dwindled, the only way to escape was to dig a new communication trench between the German and British trenches. The 1st Welsh dug towards safety, whilst the 6th Welsh Battalion, providing support, dug out to meet them. In the light, digging became suicidal as the enemy sniped and shelled the area. At some point, Arthur was hit and wounded in the elbow. By the afternoon of the 2 October, the rescue efforts were successful and the 1st Welsh were able to escape back to their own trenches. fifteen officers and 370 men were killed or wounded.

The first indication that Arthur knew he should not have been overseas is seen on the army medical forms completed during his recovery, where his age is given as nineteen: a year older than he actually was. Seven months later, Arthur was promoted to Captain and posted to the 14th Battalion who were in France. Four months later he was invalided back to England due to illness. Perhaps forgetting what age he had stated last time, or thinking he had to appear older to avoid questions about his promotion to Captain at such a young age, he said he was twenty-one, adding two years to his actual age.

Upon his recovery, he was sent out to France again, in January 1917; this time with the 15th Battalion. Only a few weeks later, on a cold February morning, Arthur was shot in the chest by a sniper. He was rushed to a casualty clearing centre but died two days later.

'Lord was a fine fellow, full of promise. He was only in the Hall a term, but it was long enough for those who came in contact with him to estimate his value. Throughout his active service he was always hopeful and cheerful, doing what he regarded as his privilege and duty in fighting the "Hun", whom he detested.' [57]

Lance Corporal

WILLIAM SPENCE

Royal Fusiliers

Hulme Hall Resident No. 406
Killed in Action 1916

Born	6 June 1895
Date Entered Hulme Hall	October 1914
Degree Course	Combined Studies
Regiment	20th and 8th Battalion Royal Fusiliers
Killed in Action	7 October 1916
Age	21
Commemorated	Theipval Memorial, Albert, France

Pre-War

Born in Hartlepool to Thomas and Emily Spence, William was educated at Galley's Field School and Henry Smith's Secondary School.

Leaving school in 1912, William accepted a job with the Hartlepool Education Committee. After successful completion of the Joint Northern Universities Matriculation exams in July 1914, he was preparing to move to Hulme Hall to study at the university at the outbreak of war.

War Service

Although William had only just turned nineteen by August 1914, he was not caught up in the fever of patriotism that swept Britain, choosing instead to continue with his studies over enlisting. As with many of his contemporaries, William joined the University OTC on arrival in Manchester, training with the unit for over a year.

It hasn't been possible to clarify what motivated William to enlist a year later in November 1915 with the 20th Battalion Royal Fusiliers. With the Derby Scheme being introduced in October, William may have felt that it was only a matter of time before he would be called upon to fight and therefore decided to do so on his own terms. A number of other Hulme Hall men enlisted in November, so he may have been influenced by their decision too.

The 20th Battalion Royal Fusiliers was formed primarily from recruits of the University Public School's Brigade who had enlisted in Manchester. The Battalion would have maintained strong links with the university, which would suggest that William had developed ties to this Battalion who had only just been posted to France in the same month as William enlisted.

William's movements after November are unclear and it has not been possible to ascertain when he arrived in France, when and why he was posted to the 8th Battalion Royal Fusiliers, or when he was appointed as a Lance Corporal.

Given the army's need for men during the Somme Offensive, which started in July 1916, it is probable that William arrived in France around this time. He would have been posted to a reinforcement depot, awaiting a call to join the Battalion when needed.

The 8th Battalion had fought earlier in the Somme Offensive than the 20th Battalion, sustaining a staggering 640 casualties out of 800 men that went into action on 7 July in the village of Ovillers. It is likely that William was diverted to the 8th Battalion in an attempt to bring the Battalion back to strength.

Whatever the reasons for his transfer, at 1.45pm on 7 October 1916 William found himself formed up in a front-line trench awaiting the order to go 'over the top'. The Battalion was to attack as part of the last official individual battle of the 1916 Somme campaign known as the Battle of Le Transloy.

Attacking alongside the 9th Battalion Royal Fusiliers, William and his comrades climbed into the mud of no man's land into a hail of enemy machine gun bullets and bursting artillery shells. It was an attack doomed to fail from the start with the enemy trenches held in greater number than anticipated. It later transpired that the attack had coincided with two German Battalions exchanging duties in their front line.

Fatally wounded, an officer stopped to bandage William's injuries. William was unable to reach the safety of his own lines in the retreat and his body was never recovered; he was one of over 100 men of the Battalion posted as missing after the engagement; a further 150 were confirmed as killed or wounded.

'An officer who helped dress his wounds writes to his parents: "Your son was a good soldier, and did his duty well. His death is felt by all his comrades, and especially by myself, his officer." He was the right stuff for a first-rate Hall man.' [58]

Private

KENNETH BARRY

Royal Fusiliers

Hulme Hall Resident No. 415
Killed in Action 1916

Born	4 June 1896
Date Entered Hulme Hall	October 1914
Degree Course	Textiles
Regiment	23rd and 30th Battalion Royal Fusiliers
Killed in Action	27 July 1916
Age	20
Commemorated	Thiepval Memorial, Albert, France

Pre-War

Kenneth was born in Coventry in 1896. He completed his secondary education at Bablake School before attending the Technical Institute in Coventry. Having successfully completed his course at the Technical Institute, Kenneth found work as a clerk in a textile works. Academically minded and keen to forge a career in the textile trade, Kenneth sat and passed the entrance exam at the School of Technology in Manchester in 1914 to complete a BSc in Textiles; a position he was preparing to take up when war was declared.

War Service

During the course of his studies, Kenneth resided at Hulme Hall. In a letter to the Warden, the Rev T Nicklin, after Kenneth was killed, his mother wrote:[59]

> During the time he was in Manchester he appeared to have been very happy at the Hall and he many times said how much he appreciated your kindness and advice whilst residing there.

That Kenneth enjoyed his time at the Hall reflected in his studies as he received First Class passes in the City and Guild of London Institute Technology examinations in 1915 for Cotton Spinning and Cotton Weaving. When starting in Manchester he also enrolled in the OTC.

After the exams Kenneth developed appendicitis and for a period was left very weak. From December 1915 he went into the works of Messrs. Levinstein, a dye firm, as a chemist. Upon recovering fully, he enlisted with the 30th Battalion Royal Fusiliers.

In June 1916 after completing his training, Private Kenneth Barry was posted to France to join A Company of the 23rd Battalion Royal Fusiliers who were operating near the Somme. Despite the Battle of the Somme raging from 1 July, the Battalion were located in a particularly quiet section of the front-line for the first ten days of the month.

As casualties began to mount, the Battalion were called upon to provide support, arriving in the Somme region on 20 July. After further training and preparation they received orders that they were to take part in an attack of Delville Wood on the morning of 27 July. There had been fierce fighting in the woods for almost two weeks, with the South African Army particularly taking severe casualties.

The initial attack was launched at 7.30am and by 9am they had captured a line fifty yards from the northern perimeter of the woods. The Battalion soon came under heavy enemy fire and counter-attack.

At some point during the subsequent fighting, Kenneth and a fellow Private, Clarence Harding, were sent back to Battalion Headquarters with an urgent message. Under heavy shelling they scrambled out of the relative safety of the trenches and made their way back across the shattered woodland through which they had just advanced. It was the last time they would be seen alive.

As Kenneth's body was never recovered, his parents duly received a telegram informing them that he had been reported as Missing in Action. It was six months before his parents received news confirming Kenneth's death, having met up with a wounded colleague of Kenneth's in hospital who confirmed he had seen him killed. [59] Kenneth's body was never recovered and his name is commemorated on the Thiepval Memorial.

'It was really hard for [Kenneth] to have to give up his studies, but I think he tried to look on the bright side of things and hoped that the time would soon come when he would be able to get back to work again.' [59]

Second Lieutenant

WILLIAM LESLIE WOOD

Royal Welsh Fusiliers

Hulme Hall Resident No. 437
Killed in Action 1917

Born	21 September 1896
Date Entered Hulme Hall	October 1915
Degree Course	Chemistry
Regiment	15th Battalion Royal Welsh Fusiliers
Killed in Action	7 May 1917
Age	20
Buried	Essex Farm Cemetery, Ypres, Belgium

Pre-War

William was born in September 1896, the third son to James and Minnie Wood. His younger sister, Dorris, was born two years later. The family lived in Leyland, to the south of Preston, where William's father was the head teacher at Leyland Church of England School.

William was educated at Balshaw's Grammar School. In 1914 he completed his secondary education, receiving a First Class Pass in the Oxford Senior Local Examinations. In October 1915 he was accepted into Hulme Hall whilst he studied Chemistry at Victoria Manchester University.

War Service

William had just turned nineteen when he arrived in Manchester and one of his first actions was to join the University OTC, applying two months later for a commission with the army. William didn't care where and with whom he served: he just wanted to join the fighting, stating on his application form that he was happy to join any branch of the army.

William only had to wait a month before being accepted, receiving news he was to report to the 11th Battalion Gloucestershire Regiment, a training Battalion who were based in Seaford.

After eight months of hard training, William was considered ready for a front-line posting and in September 1916 he was transferred to the 15th Battalion Royal Welsh Fusiliers, who had been in fighting on the Western Front since December 1915.

William was thrown straight into trench life on arrival as the Battalion were operating in the front line near the Ypres Canal in Belgium. A few weeks later, he was part of an evening raid on the German front line; the Battalion's task was to cause disruption and identify the enemy unit operating in the opposite trenches; this was his first advance into enemy territory.

Sixty-five officers, NCOs and men were selected for the raid. William was assigned to be part of the left covering party, which consisted of eight men and an NCO. It was their responsibility to protect the left flank of the two separate trench-raiding parties who would be entering the enemy lines. As this was William's first advance into no man's land, an experienced NCO was put in charge of his party. Armed with only a club, revolver and whistle, William soon found himself in command as the NCO was hit by shrapnel from British guns that were providing covering fire. The raid was a success with William and his men being the last to withdraw once the trench raiding parties had retired to the relative safety of their own lines. Twelve men were wounded with one being reported as missing.

With his confidence growing as he gained more experience, William's positive attitude marked him out to the Battalion's senior officers. In April 1917 he was appointed temporarily to the rank of Captain and put in charge of a company likely to have consisted of over 200 men.

Several weeks later, on the morning of 6 May, William's own trenches were subject to an enemy raid, which attacked under the cover of an artillery bombardment. Three men were believed to have been taken prisoner, with two being killed and a further three injured.

The next day, a moment of carelessness was to cost William his life. Exposing himself briefly he was shot by an enemy sniper. Taken to the medical station known as Essex Farm for treatment, he died later that day, being buried in the same location.

'He had been doing so well out here, and shown so much keenness and energy, that I put him in command of a company. He was put to the test the day before yesterday, when one of the trenches his company was holding was raided after bombardment by the enemy. The Brigadier General expressed great satisfaction at the way in which he handled the situation: he kept his head under very trying circumstances, and by his cheerfulness and energy restored the confidence of his company. We all feel that we have lost a very gallant young officer and a good friend.' [60]

Private

ROBERT KENNAUGH SOUTHWARD

Manchester Regiment

Hulme Hall Resident No. 439
Killed in Action 1916

Born	6 November 1896
Date Entered Hulme Hall	October 1915
Degree Course	Chemistry
Regiment	7th Battalion Manchester Regiment attached to 1st Loyal North Lancashire Regiment
Rank	Private
Killed in Action	18 August 1916
Age	19
Commemorated	Thiepval Memorial, Albert, France

Pre-War

Robert was born in November 1896 in Douglas, Isle of Man, the eldest child of William and Mary Southward. Robert had a younger sister, Winnie, who was born four years later.

Robert was educated at the Eastern District Secondary School in Douglas, where he proved to be a promising athlete, completing his studies in 1913.

War Service

Only seventeen at the outbreak of war, Robert was too young to enlist with the army, whose minimum age for fighting overseas at that time was nineteen years.

In October 1915, Robert arrived in Manchester to study Chemistry at the university. Although he was to only stay in Hulme Hall for a short period, he quickly engaged in Hall life, becoming a popular member of the community. In November, just as he turned nineteen, he joined the OTC.

On 20 January 1916, seven days before all voluntary enlistment was stopped under the Military Service Act 1916, Robert enlisted with the 7th Battalion Manchester Regiment; most likely under the Derby Scheme. He continued with his studies until March when he was called up and joined the reserve Battalion, or 2/7th Battalion, who were training in Witley Camp on Witley Common in Surrey.

There was a huge demand for manpower on the Western Front in 1916, particularly in the aftermath of the first month of the Somme Offensive. Such was the demand that whilst some Hulme Hall students who signed up in 1914 were able to train for over a year before being sent to fight, Robert received only less than five months' training, arriving in France in early August 1916. With the 1/7th Battalion serving in Sinai, Robert was attached to the 1st Battalion Loyal North Lancashire Regiment (LNLR) who were being reinforced after suffering heavy casualties during an offensive near Pozières, on the Somme, in mid-July.

Robert was to only serve with the LNLR for four days before he was killed during fighting on 18 August. His parents were informed of his death during the first week of September and the only information provided was that Robert had been killed whilst crossing no man's land.

Investigation of the 1st Battalion LNLR War Diaries for 18 August 1916 revealed that the Battalion were ordered to attack a trench running along the north-western edge of High Wood. In a report summarising the Battalion's action of the day, Major Phillips noted that at the start of the attack at 2.45pm:[61]

> The right platoon, which was detailed to attack trench X and to form a strong point at NW corner of High Wood, left their trenches and was seen to advance into our intense bombardment, which was not timed to lift until [2.48pm]. Remainder of right appears to have followed on too quickly and suffered a similar fate.

The platoons attacking to the left delayed their advance and followed successfully behind the British bombardment and took their objective. Given the limited information passed on to Robert's parents and the evidence provided in the diaries, it is considered highly likely that Robert was part of the right flank and was killed by a shell from British guns: a victim of 'friendly fire'.

'I cannot tell you how your letter of sympathy was appreciated by my parents and myself. Robert's death has indeed been a terrible blow to us all and even yet it seems hard to realise it. Father wrote almost at once to the CO of Robert's battalion for particulars. He received a reply stating that the CO was not with the company on that date but he had tried to collect a few facts. Robert was killed while crossing no man's land and he was buried on the spot where he died, which was near High Wood. That is all the information which we have at present.' [62]

Second Lieutenant

WILLIAM FREDRICK WILLIAMS

Royal Fusiliers

Hulme Hall Resident No. 444
Killed in Action 1918

Born	27 November 1897
Date Entered Hulme Hall	October 1915
Degree Course	Chemistry
Regiment	17th Battalion Royal Fusiliers
Rank	Second Lieutenant
Killed in Action	27 September 1918
Age	20
Buried	Sanders Keep Military Cemetery, Graincourt-lès-Havrincourt, France

Pre-War

It has proved difficult to uncover much personal information about William. All the usual sources that have helped to piece together the lives and stories of fellow Hulme Hall men have, for the most part, drawn a blank.

The Hulme Hall Admissions Register usually provides useful background information into a student's academic past. More often than not, the Warden would have added notes regarding the students' studies and where applicable, students' war service. However, William's page is almost bare. The register confirms that William attended Taunton School and entered Hulme Hall in October 1915 to study for a Science degree at the university, specialising in Chemistry. It is noted that William's father, John, was living in Blackpool.

The Commonwealth War Grave Commission website also provides very little information. Here, William is only recorded as W F Williams, with no additional information provided.

Surprisingly, even the Manchester University Roll of Service does not record the fact that William was killed. His entry simply records that he was a student at the university, a member of the OTC and served with the Royal Fusiliers. A further search shows that William's name is missing from the University War Memorial and the Taunton School Memorial.

War Service

William would have been seventeen years old when he first arrived at Hulme Hall in 1915, still too young to enlist. As he was quick to join the University OTC, he would have been in a good position to receive a commission with the army once he had turned nineteen.

The first trace of William having joined the army was found in the war diaries of the 17th Battalion Royal Fusiliers which record that a Second Lieutenant W F Williams joined the Battalion in April 1918, alongside eleven other officers.

In March, the month prior to William joining the 17th Battalion in France, the German Army launched their Spring Offensive, considered to be a last effort at forcing a victory on the Western Front before the arrival, in strength, of American forces. The 17th Battalion Royal Fusiliers were rotated out of the front line on the evening of 20 March, the eve of the offensive, but a few days later were involved in an attempt to hold back the tide of the attack, suffering over 375 casualties in the process.

May was much quieter for the Battalion, giving them a chance to regroup and integrate new officers and men. After several days in the front-line trenches, the remainder of the month was spent in rest and training. Two American officers were attached for training, whilst all officers were reminded of the need to raise morale amongst the men; singing whilst marching being one of the suggested ways this could be achieved. The Battalion also competed in inter-Battalion sporting and army competitions.

By August, the German attack had faltered and the Allies exploited the fact, driving the enemy back. William and the 17th Battalion were involved in the advance and were subject to a mustard gas attack at the end of the month that caused over ninety casualties.

The Battalion continued to advance throughout September, and by the end of the month they had moved forward almost thirty miles from their original position in August. On 27 September, the Battalion were involved in the opening attacks of a battle around the incomplete Canal du Nord on the outskirts of Cambrai. Moving up from their trenches in the early hours, William and his men reached their first objective, Lock 7, on the canal by 9am. Shortly after their arrival, an enemy aeroplane flew over the canal and dropped bombs, three of which scored direct hits on the canal, killing William and three of his men.

William's mother, Sarah, died in 1900 just months before his third birthday. Sarah is buried in Crompton Cemetery, Oldham. Although William is buried in France, his name is remembered on his mother's grave.

SECTION 2

Hulme Hall men who were killed or died during the First World War and are not remembered on the War Memorial

The accounts of the men are ordered according to the date they arrived at Hulme Hall

Captain

WILLIAM BARNETT WARRINGTON

Royal Army Medical Corps

Hulme Hall Resident No. 12
Died of Illness 1919

Born	11 May 1869
Date Entered Hulme Hall	September 1887
Degree Course	Medicine
Regiment	Royal Army Medical Corps
Died of Illness	2 February 1919
Age	49
Buried	Liverpool (Anfield) Cemetery, Liverpool, England

Pre-War

William Barnett was born in May 1869 in Liverpool to John and Margaret Warrington. John Warrington was a successful cheese merchant in Liverpool.

William was one of eleven children to John. William's mother, Margaret, was John's second wife. John and Margaret had married in 1855, a year after the death of his first wife, Eliza, with whom he had two children. Sadly, Margaret died in 1871. John remarried several years later and had six further children with his new wife, also called Margaret.

William was educated at Wesley College in Sheffield. In July 1886 he successfully completed the London Intermediate BSc but failed in the examinations of a BSc a year later in 1887. Undeterred, William applied and was accepted to study Medicine at Owens College, winning the Dauntesey Medical Scholarship. William was only the twelfth resident through the doors of the newly reopened Hulme Hall when moving to Manchester in September 1887.

William remained at Hulme Hall for a year, moving out in July 1888. He proved a talented student of Medicine, firstly completing the Manchester Bachelor of Medicine, Bachelor of Surgery degree in 1891 and the London Bachelor of Medicine degree two years later in 1893.

Between 1893 and 1896 William found work as a house doctor at Manchester Royal Infirmary, City of London Hospital for Diseases of the Chest and the National Hospital for the Paralysed and Epileptic before undertaking research in neurology in Leipzig, Germany. In 1896, he continued to study neurology whilst setting up a medical practice in Liverpool.

Between 1896 and 1914, William continued to build a successful career in Medicine, becoming a recognised authority on nervous diseases, publishing work on the anatomy of nerve cells. He was appointed as Assistant Physician to the Stanley Hospital and the Hospital for Consumption; later a Physician to the Northern Hospital and Assistant Physician to the Liverpool Royal Infirmary. He also lectured on neuropathology at Liverpool University.

William was married in 1899 to Annie Alexandria Weeks in London. They had three children: Phyllis, Reginald and William.

War Service

In July 1907 William was commissioned into the newly formed Territorial Army with the rank of Captain, and was mobilised onto the staff into the 1st Western General Hospital, based in Liverpool, for the duration of the war.

In an obituary published in the British Medical Journal, it was recorded that at the outbreak of war in 1914, William found scope for indefatigable work on the various nerve lesions and their results among the wounded [63]. Although his name is not on the Hulme Hall War Memorial, William is remembered on the University of Manchester War Memorial.

'As a physician Dr Warrington was in the front rank in all that related to nervous disease. He possessed in an eminent degree the contemplative trend of mind. The more intricate the problem the more attractive it was to him. He pondered deeply over his cases, and by his sound knowledge and clinical acumen often shed light on what was previously obscure and uncertain.

By nature modest and impressed by the enormous gaps in neurological knowledge, Dr Warrington was over insistent on this point in the numerous papers he has published, and whenever he spoke at the Medical Institution. He took wide views, and it could never be said that in his study of disease his outlook was cramped.' [63]

Second Lieutenant

DUDLEY COLLINS FRANCIS

Royal Fusiliers and York and Lancaster Regiment

Hulme Hall Resident No. 214
Killed in Action 1916

Born	30 July 1887
Date Entered Hulme Hall	October 1903
Degree Course	Engineering
Regiment	18th Bn. Royal Fusiliers & 5th Bn. York and Lancaster
Killed in Action	13 November 1916
Age	29
Buried	Hebuterne Military Cemetery, Pas de Calais, France

Pre-War

Dudley Collins was the second child, and only son, born to Harry and Alice Francis. Harry Francis was a Civil Engineer, and it was in these footsteps that Dudley was to follow. Raised in Devonport and educated at Plymouth College, Dudley arrived at Manchester and Hulme Hall to study engineering having just turned sixteen years of age.

The demands for studying for a degree at a young age proved too much for Dudley, and, having failed in his preliminary examinations twice within his first year, the Hulme Hall Warden recommended that he be removed from university due to his age and academic ability.

Dudley returned to Devonport and started working as an apprentice under his father, becoming his assistant in 1910. A year later he moved to South Africa where he was appointed as an assistant to the Chief Engineer of the Rand Water Board in Johannesburg and by 1912 was elected as an Associate Member of the Institute of Civil Engineers.

War Service

Dudley took to life in South Africa and only returned to England in October 1914 at the outbreak of war, enlisting with the University and Public Schools (UPS) Brigade at their recruitment office in Plymouth. Attached to the 1st Battalion UPS, who later became the 18th Battalion Royal Fusiliers (UPS), Dudley began training in Epsom.

The beginning of November 1915 proved an exciting time as the Battalion prepared to be mobilised to France. New equipment was received and training intensified. Courses included instruction in entrenching, sandbag revetments, bayonet fighting, judging distance, rapid loading, wire entanglement and bomb throwing amongst other subjects. Parades and inspections followed; the most notable was an inspection by the Queen on Salisbury Plain.

In the early hours of 14 November, the Battalion left Tidworth for Folkestone where they embarked on HMS *Princess Victoria*. Although arriving in Boulogne Harbour by 11.15am, it wasn't until early evening that they were able to disembark owing to the threat of mines. As there were no offensives that winter, Dudley and the Battalion did not go 'over the top' during the following three months, although casualties still occurred on a regular basis.

The demand for officers in the British Army by early 1916 was becoming critical and Dudley, along with many of his colleagues, were given the opportunity to apply for a commission. In February, Dudley returned to England to begin officer training. Such were the numbers being granted commissions; the Battalion was disbanded in France two months later.

Dudley responded well to the demands of training and in July 1916 was appointed as a Second Lieutenant. Two months later he was attached to the 5th York and Lancaster Battalion, arriving on the front line near Thiepval Wood, on the Somme, in early September. Dudley's new Battalion had been fighting on the Somme since the 1st July and had suffered over 300 casualties within the first week. On the day after his arrival, Dudley's positions were bombarded from 2.30am until dawn with gas. Over 110 men became casualties.

As the Battle of the Somme came to a close, the Allies launched a final attack on 13 November, on and around the River Ancre. Dudley's company was ordered to assist other Battalions involved in the attack by laying a smoke barrage. Assisted by an early morning mist, the task was successful. Despite not retaliating whilst the smoke screen was being laid, German artillery later began heavily shelling Dudley's position and he was killed by shrapnel whilst sheltering in a communication trench.

30% of men reinforcing his Battalion in September 1916 were found to have had less than three months' military service before arriving in France [64]. *Having experienced almost two years of army service, including four months of life on the front line, Dudley would have had to work hard to bring the men under his command up to scratch.*

Captain

ARTHUR RAYMOND MARSHALL

Royal Navy Division / Royal Garrison Artillery

Hulme Hall Resident No. 284
Died of Wounds 1918

Born	3 October 1890
Date Entered Hulme Hall	October 1908
Degree Course	Mathematics
Regiment	Royal Navy Division / Royal Garrison Artillery
Died of Wounds	2 February 1918
Age	27
Buried	St Sever Cemetery, Rouen, France

Pre-War

Arthur Raymond was born in Bengal, India, to Charles and Lucy Marshall in 1890. At the time Charles was manager of the Bengal Silk Company Ltd. The family later returned to Bathford, a village to the north-east of Bath.

In September 1904 Arthur started at Marlborough College, having received a scholarship. Here he shone academically, being described as having an energy, characterised 'as akin to genius'.[65]

Whilst at Marlborough, Arthur developed a keen interest in engineering. Such was his passion for the subject that in 1908, he gave up his last year at Marlborough to undertake a private course in Mathematics at Victoria University of Manchester.

During the year course, he lived at Hulme Hall. Afterwards he headed to Cambridge University to study Mechanical Science for four years at Cains College. Having completed his degree, he started an apprenticeship with Belliss & Morcom, an engineering company based in Birmingham.

Having served in the Marlborough College and Manchester University OTC, Arthur continued his military training by joining the King Edward's Horse at Cambridge, a cavalry regiment, serving for two years between 1911 and 1913.

War Service

In September 1914 Arthur enlisted with the Royal Marines Engineers and was appointed as a dispatch rider with 99th Signal Company with the newly formed Royal Naval Division (RND). He was promoted to the rank of Corporal the following month.

In early 1915 the RND was mobilised to Egypt where they began training to take part in the assault of Gallipoli. Arthur would have been amongst the first waves of troops arriving on the beaches of Gallipoli in April. Having survived the majority of the unsuccessful campaign unscathed, Arthur was evacuated to the island of Lemnos in November 1915 having contracted dysentery, only a month before the army retreated.

Arthur rejoined his unit in January 1916. Four months later, the RND were transferred to the Western Front, arriving in Marseilles. The RND were assigned responsibility for a section of the front line near Arras, which was relatively quiet for the majority of 1916. Arthur continued to distinguish himself in his work and in mid-1916, he was accepted for officer training, leaving for England in September, perhaps for the first time since he had left for Egypt in early 1915.

Commissioned into the Royal Garrison Artillery (RGA), Arthur joined the 118th Siege Battalion in February 1917 in France. Within a month he was posted to the Head Quarters of the 34th Heavy Artillery Group (HAG). Arthur proved effective in his work, being promoted to Captain in October and assigned as Adjutant, responsible for administration of the HAG.

In November, Arthur was granted leave for two weeks, returning just as the Battle of Cambrai began. On 8 December, whilst undertaking a reconnaissance, Arthur was severely wounded in the right leg by an enemy shell that exploded nearby. Two months later, Arthur succumbed to his injuries at the Red Cross Hospital in Rouen, being buried with military honours.

Due to the life-threatening nature of his wounds, Arthur's next of kin, his uncle Arthur Peters, was given permission by the army to travel to France to visit him. Appointing his wife to go in his place, Beatrice Peters was able to visit Arthur before his death. [66]

Private

FRANK CLARE CARESS

Cheshire Regiment

Hulme Hall Resident No. 321
Died of Illness 1918

Born	20 July 1889
Date Entered Hulme Hall	October 1910
Degree Course	Engineering
Regiment	5th Battalion Cheshire Regiment
Died of Illness	20 October 1918
Age	29
Buried	Unknown

Pre-War

Frank Clare was born in Northwich, Cheshire, the third of four children, and only son, to Herbert and Annie Caress. Herbert was the headmaster of the local elementary school.

Frank attended Winnington Park School. After the death of his mother in 1901, he attended Wilton Grammar School and then Elstow School in Bedford, where he was a member of the School OTC.

After completing his secondary education, Frank returned to Northwich before sitting and passing the entrance examination to Victoria University of Manchester in September 1910 at the age of twenty-one. A month later he started a degree in Engineering, residing at Hulme Hall. Struggling academically, Frank failed the intermediate examinations in July 1911 and July 1912, leaving the university shortly after the second failed attempt.

Upon returning to Northwich, Frank found work as a Civil Engineer with the River Weaver Navigation Trustees.

War Service

On 8 August 1914, four days after Great Britain declared war on Germany, Frank enlisted with the 5th Battalion Cheshire Regiment in Chester. The 5th Battalion were a Territorial Army unit who were mobilised for full-time service when war was declared.

The Territorial Army were primarily a home defence force, with service outside of the United Kingdom only required in a national emergency. On 14 September Frank signed a release form stating that he was willing to serve overseas.

By the end of August, the Battalion had moved to Northampton for training. In December they were moved to Cambridge where they began to prepare for mobilisation to the Western Front.

Although Frank got through almost six months of training, his health failed him and at the beginning of 1915 he was medically discharged from the army on the grounds of problems with his vision. It was noted on his discharge papers that he was also anaemic which was impacting and affecting his performance.

Only two weeks after was discharged, the 5th Battalion sailed for France. Seeing his friends and colleagues sailing off to war after six months together must have been difficult for Frank to deal with.

His whereabouts for the next two years has not been confirmed, but at some point Frank found work as an engineer on the SS *Irishman*, with the Atlantic Transport Line. Although not militaristic, this line of work was dangerous, particularly as the German Navy relaunched an unrestrictive submarine campaign on all shipping in the Atlantic in 1917. During the course of the war four Atlantic Transport Line-owned ships were sunk.

In June 1918 Frank married Florence May Shilliday in Northwich. Only four months later, he died at Greenwich Seamen's Hospital from pneumonia after an illness contracted whilst serving on the SS *Irishman*.

The Greenwich Seamen's Hospital was founded by the Seamen's Hospital Society in 1821 in response to the increasing number of homeless and impoverished seafarers living on the streets of London after the Napoleonic wars. The Society formed a committee to fit out and run a floating hospital ship. In 1870 the hospital came ashore and operated for over 100 years from the former Greenwich Hospital Infirmary.

Reverend J H Hopkinson
John Henry Hopkinson served as Warden at Hulme Hall whilst a lecturer in Archaeology at the University, leaving both in 1914 at the age of 38 to be ordained. Author's own collection.

Reverend Thomas Nicklin
Reverend Thomas Nicklin served as Warden of Hulme Hall for 23 years, from the start of the First World War in 1914 until 1937. Author's own collection.

Cloisters in the North Court
Undated postcard of Hulme Hall. Author's own collection.

Tower and Gateway of Houldsworth building
Undated postcard of Houldsworth building, Hulme Hall. Author's own collection.

Hulme Hall 2016

Old Meets New – The historic Old Dinning Room sits against the new dinning room and administration offices. Author's own collection.

Hulme Hall 2016

Old Meets New – The original 1907 Holdsworth building with Birley block, built in the in 1960s, in the background. Author's own collection.

Howard Harker's Royal Aero Club Aviator Certificate

18 months after the outbreak of war, Howard Harker was finally able to achieve his goal of fighting for his country. Howard completed his pilot training with the RFC in May 1916, being awarded his Aviator Certificate by the Royal Aero Club. Courtesy of The Royal Aero Club Trust.

2945

HARKER, Howard Redmayne
Assize Courts, Manchester

Born 12th May 1891 *at* Prestwich, Manchester
Nationality British
Rank, Regiment, Profession 2nd Lieut. R.F.C.(S.R.)
Certificate taken on Maurice Farman Biplane
At Military School, Birmingham
Date 18th May 1916

Harry Pickles
Although able to apply for a commission, former Senior Student Harry Pickles (left) felt compelled to enlist as a Private to gain an appreciation of the life and lot of a solider. This photo was taken with a friend whilst training at Frensham Camp in November 1914. Courtesy of Susan Pares.

Wilfred Trevelyan (Left) and James Henderson (Right)

The story of friends Wilfred Trevelyan (left) and James Henderson (right) captures the indiscriminate nature of life in the trenches. Both arrived in France together with the Rifle Brigade in April 1915. A month later, Wilfred was fatality wounded by shrapnel whilst repairing a communication trench. Henderson went on to become a veteran of the front-line, being wounded twice before being killed in August 1916 after capturing an enemy machine-gun single handed during the Battle of the Somme. Author's own collection (Trevelyan). Courtesy of The University of Manchester (Henderson).

Menin Gate Memorial (above) and Inscription (below)
Originally buried in the grounds of Hooge Chateau near Ypres, Wilfred's body was not recovered after the war. Wilfred is one of over 54,000 men remembered on the Menin Gate Memorial who have no known grave. Fellow Hulme Hall resident Harold Danby Swift is also remembered on the Menin Gate. Author's own collection.

Grave of James G M Henderson

James' body was recovered after he was killed during an attack at Guillemont Station during the Battle of the Somme. He is buried in Delville Wood Cemetery, Longueval. Author's own collection.

Thiepval Memorial
The imposing Thiepval Memorial was completed in 1932 to remember the names of over 72,240 men who served in the British and Commonwealth Armies who died in the region of the Somme and who have no known grave. The names of eight Hulme Hall men are recorded on the Memorial. Author's own collection.

Charles Hamilton Murray Chapman
Taken from his Aviator Certificate, this photo of Murray Chapman appears to perfectly capture his character. Murray survived several crashes before being killed during a collision with another aircraft whilst escorting an airship in 1918. Courtesy of The Royal Aero Club Trust.

Drawings of Dinosaurs

A talented artist, Murray wrote and illustrated a children's book before the war, which was published by his family after his death. C H Murray Chapman, Dragons at Home (Wells Gardner, Darton & Co. Ltd, undated).

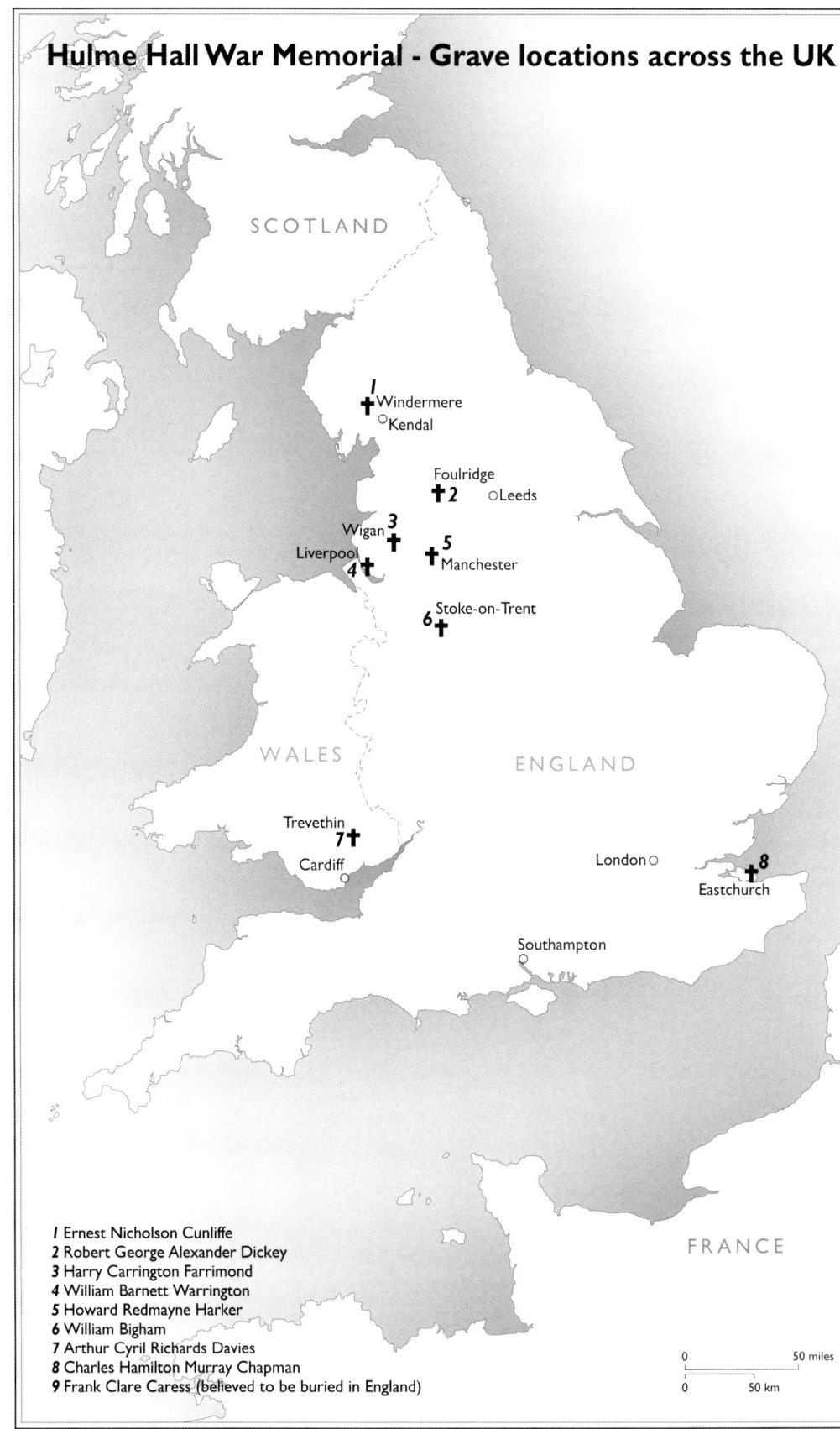

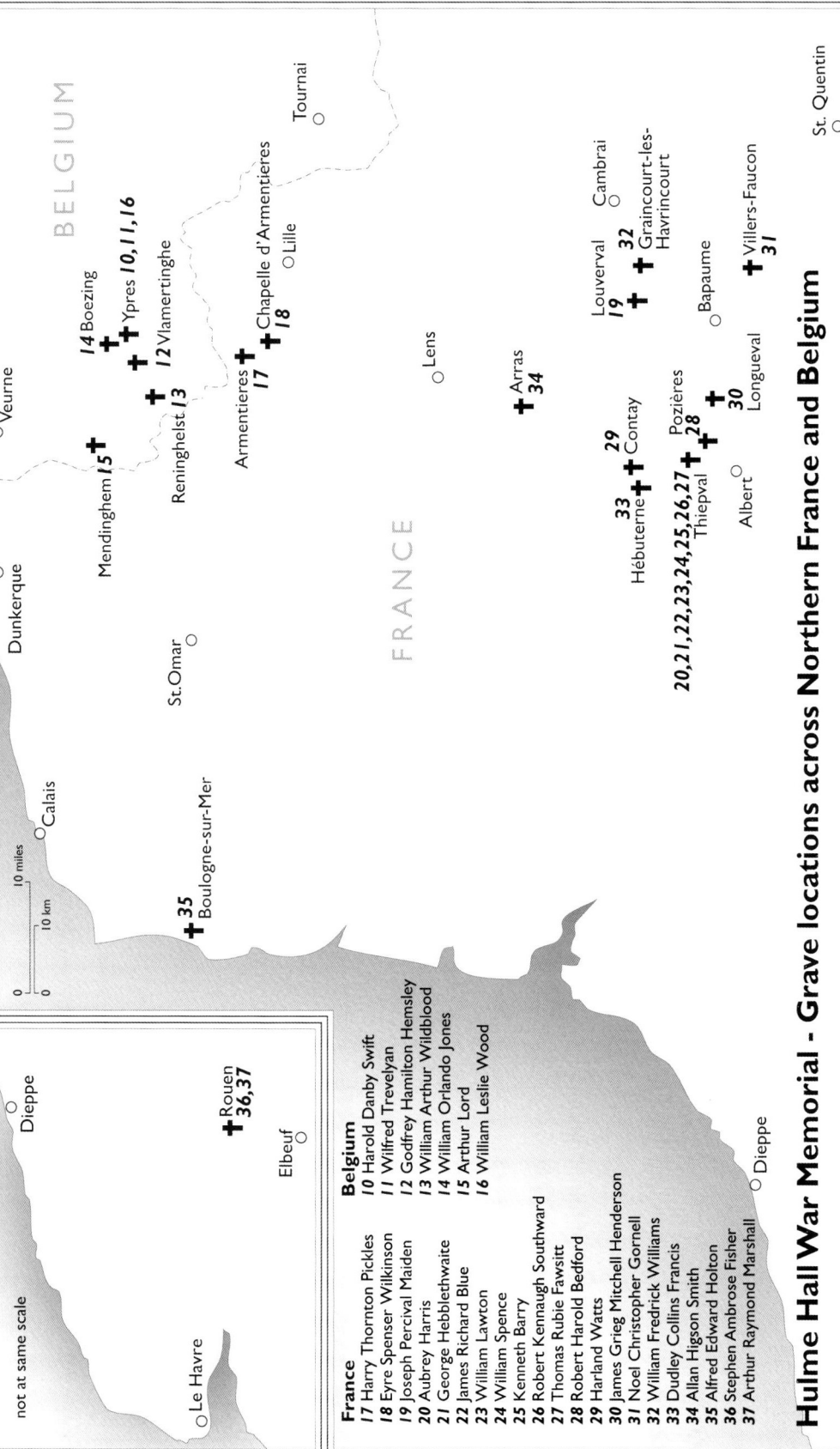

United Kingdom

1. Ernest Nicholson Cunliffe — St Mary's Church, Windermere, LA23 1BA
2. Robert George Alexander Dickey — St Michael's Church, Foulridge, Lancashire, BB8 7PY
3. Harry Carrington Farrimond — Wigan Cemetery, Wigan, WN3 4NL
4. William Barnett Warrington — Liverpool (Anfield) Cemetery, Liverpool, L4 2SL
5. Howard Redmayne Harker — Manchester Southern Cemetery, Manchester, M21 7GL
6. William Bigham — Stoke-on-Trent (Hartshill) Cemetery, Stoke-on-Trent, ST4 7LH
7. Arthur Cyril Richards Davies — St Cadoc Churchyard, Trevethin, Monmouthshire, NP4 8JF
8. Charles Hamilton Murray Chapman — All Saints Church, Eastchurch, Isle of Sheppey, ME12 4BN
9. Frank Clare Caress — Unknown, believed to be buried in England

Belgium

10. Harold Danby Swift — Menin Gate Memorial, Ypres
11. Wilfred Trevelyan — Menin Gate Memorial, Ypres
12. Godfrey Hamilton Hemsley — Vlamertinghe New Military Cemetery, Vlamertinghe
13. William Arthur Wildblood — Reninghelst New Military Cemetery, Reninghelst
14. William Orlando Jones — Bards Cottage Cemetery, Boezinge
15. Arthur Lord — Mendinghem Military Cemetery, Mendinghem
16. William Leslie Wood — Essex Farm Cemetery, Ypres

France

17. Harry Thornton Pickles — Cite bongean Military Cemetery, Armentieres
18. Eyre Spenser Wilkinson — Chapelle D'Aarmentieres New Military Cemetery
19. Joseph Percival Maiden — Cambrai Memorial, Louverval
20. Aubrey Harris — Thiepval Memorial, Thiepval
21. George Hebblethwaite — Thiepval Memorial, Thiepval
22. James Richard Blue — Thiepval Memorial, Thiepval
23. William Lawton — Thiepval Memorial, Thiepval
24. William Spence — Thiepval Memorial, Thiepval
25. Kenneth Barry — Thiepval Memorial, Thiepval
26. Robert Kennaugh Southward — Thiepval Memorial, Thiepval
27. Thomas Rubie Fawsitt — Thiepval Memorial, Thiepval
28. Robert Harold Bedford — Pozières Memorial, Pozières
29. Harland Watts — Contay Military Cemetery, Contay
30. James Grieg Mitchell Henderson — Delville Wood Cemetery, Longueval
31. Noel Christopher Gornell — villers-Faucon Communal Cemetery Exension, Villers-Faucon
32. William Fredrick Williams — Sanders Keep Military Cemetery, Graincourt-les-Havrincourt
33. Dudley Collins Francis — Hebuterne Military Cemetery, Pas de Calais
34. Allan Higson Smith — Arras Flying Services Memorial, Arras
35. Alfred Edward Holton — Terlincthun British Cemetery, Boulogne
36. Stephen Ambrose Fisher — St Sever Cemetery, Rouen
37. Arthur Raymond Marshall — St Sever Cemetery, Rouen

Other Countries

38. William George Freemantle — Helles Memorial, Gallipoli
29. Harold James Porter — Alexandria (Chatby) Military Cemetery, Egypt
30. Arthur Morton Goodall — Moshi Cemetery, Moshi, Tanzania

Second Lieutenant
THOMAS RUBIE FAWSITT

Middlesex Regiment and York and Lancaster Regiment

Hulme Hall Resident No. 322
Killed in Action 1916

Born	15 March 1886
Date Entered Hulme Hall	October 1910
Degree Course	Medicine
Regiment	16th Battalion Middlesex Regiment, 3rd and 9th Battalions York & Lancaster Regiment
Killed in Action	16 September 1916
Age	30
Commemorated	Thiepval Memorial, Albert, France

Pre-War

Thomas was born in March 1886 in Oldham, the eldest son of Dr Thomas Fawsitt and his wife Eliza.

A border at both Aysgarth School in Yorkshire and Shrewsbury School, Thomas also attended Closelet School in Lausanne, Switzerland, before entering Christ's College in Cambridge in October 1905.

At Christ's College Thomas distinguished himself as a coxswain, breaking into the College squad in his first year. He went on to act as cox for three years, leading the College's eight-man team to victory in the Thames Cup at Henley in 1906 and 1907. The fact that he had poor eyesight and had to wear glasses was thought to have prevented him from representing the university.

In 1908 Thomas left Cambridge, later being accepted at Victoria University of Manchester to study Medicine. At the start of his third year in October 1910, he moved into Hulme Hall. However, his work ethic did not match that expected of him and he left the university in March 1911. Luton was the next stop as he found work at the Vauxhall Motor Works as a Motor Engineer. Thomas also went into business, becoming a partner in Geo. Ward, Fawsitt and Co. Ltd although this venture did not succeed and the company was liquidated in September 1912.

Struggling to find direction in his life, Thomas moved to Cambridge House in Camberwell, a charity founded by Cambridge University students to tackle poverty in London. Although untrained in the work, and despite a very different upbringing, Thomas found he had a natural ability to connect with those he met. Having found a sense of purpose in his involvement with Cambridge House, he stayed there until the outbreak of war in August 1914.

War Service

Caught in the excitement that gripped much of the country, Thomas was quick to enlist with the 16th Middlesex (Public School) Battalion in early September 1914. He was promoted to Corporal in January 1915 shortly after beginning the process of applying for a commission. Perhaps feeling that being an NCO was affecting his chances of attending officer training, Thomas reverted back to the rank of Private at his own request two months later.

Thomas was finally accepted for officer training, being commissioned as Second Lieutenant with the 3rd Battalion York and Lancaster Regiment in June 1915. Initially based in Sunderland, the Battalion moved to Durham in August, forming part of the Tyne Garrison. In February 1916 Thomas was involved in an accident whilst cleaning out his billets, fracturing his elbow, requiring two months' sick leave before being considered fit enough to resume training.

With the British Army suffering heavy casualties at the start of the Somme Offensive in July 1916, Thomas was sent to France, being attached to the 9th Battalion at the end of July. His first experiences being in the front line came two weeks later, with the majority of time being taken repairing trenches and rewiring weakened sections of their defences.

On the evening of 15 September, the Battalion were moved up to Push Alley, a new front-line trench, after a successful attack on the village of Martinpuich. The next day they established two strong advance posts. Subject to counter-attacks and continued shelling through the day, Thomas was killed, one of thirty-seven casualties suffered by the Battalion that day.

Cambridge House is still in operation today. The charity continues to focus on working with vulnerable families and communities, using their expertise and knowledge to tackle the root causes of poverty. [67]

Lieutenant

HARRY CARRINGTON FARRIMOND

Royal Fusiliers and East Lancashire Regiment

Hulme Hall Resident No. 407
Died of Illness 1919

Born	24 September 1895
Date Entered Hulme Hall	October 1914
Degree Course	Ordinary BSc
Regiment	18th / 10th Bn. Royal Fusiliers and East Lancashire Regiment, Nottingham and Derbyshire Regiment
Died of Illness	14 March 1919
Age	23
Buried	Wigan Cemetery, Wigan, England

Pre-War

Harry Carrington was born in Ashton-in-Makerfield in 1895, the only child of William and Ellen Farrimond. William worked as a coal miner hewer at the local coal mine.

Harry attended Ashton-in-Makerfield Grammar School, passing the Joint Northern University Matriculation examinations at the age of seventeen in 1913. In October 1914 he began an Ordinary BSc degree at Victoria University of Manchester, residing at Hulme Hall.

War Service

As with many of his contemporaries who started university in the autumn of 1914, Harry joined the University OTC on his arrival in Manchester, enlisting with the 18th Battalion Royal Fusiliers (1st Public School Battalion) after his first year when it became apparent the war was not likely to end quickly and the need for new recruits had intensified.

After six months' training, during which time he was appointed Lance Corporal, Harry embarked to France to join the Battalion in January 1916. With the demand for officers growing as casualties continued to mount, the 18th Battalion was disbanded in April due to the number of men being accepted for officer training. As a result, Harry and fifty-three other men were posted to the 10th Battalion Royal Fusiliers, arriving in May just after their new colleagues had returned to trenches near Berles-au-Bois to the south-west of Arras.

The 10th Battalion were based near Berles-au-Bois for two months, during which time both sides were active in patrolling, sniping and machine gunning of their opponent's trenches.

In early July the 10th Battalion were ordered from Berles-au-Bois to the Somme to support the offensive which had started so disastrously on 1 July. Arriving near Albert by motorised vehicles, the Battalion made their way forward towards the frontline, passing at one stage over 500 German prisoners of war. The prisoners were demoralised and in a miserable condition having suffered under an intense bombardment for several days. Harry also marched past the foreboding sight of men who had been killed during early engagements being buried. Casualties were particularly heavy at this point as men had been caught by enemy machine-gun crossfire.

On the 15 July the Battalion were engaged in supporting an attack on the village of Pozières. Coming under heavy machine-gun fire, Harry was wounded. Able to fall back to receive treatment, he was considered to be wounded badly enough to be evacuated back to England a week later.

In September Harry was posted to the 6th Battalion Royal Fusiliers, based in Dover, to continue rehabilitation. A month later, he applied, and was accepted, for officer training, receiving a commission with the East Lancashire Regiment in May 1917.

After a spell training with the 3rd Battalion near Newcastle, Harry was posted to the 9th Battalion in Salonika, Greece. Harry served here for seven months before being evacuated back to England in March 1918 having contracted malaria and being hospitalised on a number of occasions. Upon recovery he was posted to the Nottingham and Derbyshire Regiment.

Harry was demobilised from the army at Heaton Park, Manchester in January 1919. Only two months later he fell ill again, succumbing to influenza and hyperpyrexia in March.

Considered to have died of natural causes after his demobilisation, Harry's family did not receive a memorial plaque and scroll which were given to the family of men and women who died during the war. In October 1923, his parents successfully appealed against this decision, arguing that his death was the direct result of malaria contracted during military service.

'I am directed to inform you that the Officers' Appeal Tribunal allowed, on the ground of aggravation, the appeal of the mother of Second Lieutenant H C Farrimond, East Lancashire Regiment, against the decision of this Department that the late officer's death was neither attributable to or aggravated by his military service during the Great War.' [68]

Second Lieutenant

NOEL CHRISTOPHER GORNELL

Royal Engineers

Hulme Hall Resident – Scholar Elect
killed in Action 1918

Born	27 December 1897
Date Entered Hulme Hall	Scholar Elect
Resident Number	-
Degree Course	Engineering
Regiment	157th Field Company, Royal Engineers
Killed in Action	21 March 1918
Age	20
Buried	Villers-Faucon, the Somme, France

Pre-War

Noel was born in Portsmouth, the eldest child to his parents Christopher and Annie Gornell.

Christopher Gornell was born in 1862, joining the army in 1876 at the age of fourteen. He was still in the army when Noel was born in 1897, being posted to Ireland shortly afterwards. Noel was initially educated in Ireland. After Christopher was discharged from the army, the family moved to Lancashire where Noel attended Lancaster Royal Grammar School.

Noel proved to be talented both in his studies and on the sports fields where he excelled particularly at cricket, playing for the school 1st XI between 1915 and 1917. Noel was also appointed School Captain and a House Prefect.

Only sixteen years of age at the outbreak of war, Noel joined his school OTC unit in September 1914. By early 1917 he had been promoted to Sergeant and put in charge of a platoon of his peers. Whilst still at Lancaster Royal Grammar School, Noel applied and was accepted to study Engineering at Victoria University of Manchester, winning a scholarship at Hulme Hall.

War Service

As with so many of his generation, Noel's plans were put on hold by the war. Having demonstrated leadership ability with the OTC, his Commanding Officer recommended he apply for a commission into the infantry. Submitting his application in March 1917, he expressed a preference to join either the Royal Engineers or King's Own Lancaster Regiment.

A month later in April, Noel received orders to report to the Royal Engineer base at Newark where he started officer training. Four months later he successfully completed the course, receiving a commission as a Second Lieutenant, and was posted to the strength of the 100th Field Company Royal Engineers. With the 100th Field Company in Macedonia, Noel remained in England, undertaking further training. In December, he received orders to join the 157th Field Company who were serving with the 16th (Irish) Division south of Arras, in France, providing technical skills to fighting units.

In January 1918, the 157th Field Company moved further south near Villers-Faucon, within the Somme region. Working in the reserve area, the month was uneventful, with only a warning of an enemy gas attack, which proved to be a false alarm, causing excitement.

February and the majority of March proved to be equally mundane. Towards the end of February, the Division put into practice the Villers-Faucon defence scheme, a plan that would prove to be wholly inadequate less than a month later.

On 21 March, the German Army launched their massive Spring Offensive in an effort to win the war before the Allied Forces could be successfully reinforced with the newly arriving American Army. At 4.30am on the 21 March, the village of Villers-Faucon came under an intense bombardment. The 157th Field Company were withdrawn to the west of the village, whilst a portion of the company, thought to include Noel, were sent back to dig new positions in an effort to hold Villers-Faucon. Holding on until the evening, the whole 157th Field Company were withdrawn from the front line to regroup. At some point during the day, Noel was killed.

The German Army swept through Villers-Faucon the next day. The following week, Noel's body was recovered by the Germans and buried in the village. They notified the British Army of his death via the Geneva Red Cross.

A talented cricketer, Noel's death was reported in Wisden Cricketers' Almanack. His name is included in the book Wisden on the Great War: The Lives of Cricket's Fallen 1914–1918. *Unfortunately, no records of Noel's endeavours on the cricket pitch for Lancaster Royal Grammar School were recorded in Wisden.*

BIBLIOGRAPHY, SOURCES AND ENDNOTES

Good reading material is the one thing lacking here. I would give a sovereign for any of those history text books into which I dipped only too seldom in those happy three years I spent in the history school. I have to spend still another year at the university when I get back, so that I hope to take up the threads again.

Lieutenant Robert Bedford, Gallipoli – October 1915

Hulme Hall 1912–1914

BIBLIOGRAPHY

The following books and websites have helped to develop my understanding of the First World War in general and the battles and situations individual Hulme Hall men found themselves in.

Books

William Brockbank, *The Honorary Medical Staff of the Manchester Royal Infirmary 1830–1948 (Manchester University Press, 1965)*

Lieutenant W Meakin, *History of the 5th North Staffords and the North Midland Territorials (the 46th and 59th Divisions), 1914–1919* (Hughes and Harber Limited, undated)

Gerald B Hurst, *With Manchesters in the East* (The Naval & Military Press Ltd, undated)

Yorkshire Rugby Football Union, *Commemoration Book 1914–19 and Official Handbook Season 1919–20* (published by Authority, 1919)

Peter Hart, *Bloody April – Slaughter in the Skies Over Arras, 1917* (Cassell, 2006)

Jon Guttman, *Reconnaissance and Bomber Aces of World War I* (Osprey Publishing, 2015)

Norman Franks and Hal Giblin, *Under the Guns of the German Aces* (Grub Street, 1997)

C H Murray Chapman, *Dragons at Home* (Wells Gardner, Darton & Co. Ltd, undated)

The History of the Royal Fusiliers 'UPS' University and Public Schools Brigade (The Times, undated)

Ian Connerty, Sir Martin Gilbert, Peter Hart, Lyn MacDonald and Nigel Steel *At the Going Down of the Sun – 365 Soldiers from the Great War* (Lannoo, 2001)

Michael Stedman, *Manchester Pals* (Leo Cooper, 2004)

John Hartley, *6th Battalion The Manchester Regiment in the Great War* (Pen & Sword Military, 2010)

Terry Norman, *The Hell they Called High Wood* (Pen & Sword Military, 2012)

Captain Reginald Berkley and Brigadier-General William W Seymour, *The History of The Rifle Brigade in the War of 1914–1918 Volume 1 and Volume 2* (N & M Press, 2003)

John Lewis-Stempel, *Six Weeks* (Orion Books Ltd, 2010)

Colne and District Roll of Honour and War Record 1914–1919 (Colne and Nelson Times, 1920)

Steven Howarth, *A Grammar School at War – the Story of Ermysted's Grammar School during the Great War* (John Mason, 2007)

Lieutenant-Colonel W A V Churton, DSO *1/5th Earl of Chester's Battalion 1914–1919* (The Naval & Military Press Ltd, undated)

Susan Pares, *Displaced by War* (Francis Boutle Publishers, 2015)

E P F Lynch, *Somme Mud* (Bantam Books, 2008)

Ian Mackersey, *No Empty Chairs* (Phoenix, 2013)

Sir J A Hammerton, *A Popular History of the Great War; Volumes 1 to 6* (The Amalgamated Press, Ltd, undated)

Alan Clark, *The Donkeys* (Hutchinson & Co. Ltd, 1961)

Geoff D Copeman, *Bomber Squadrons at War* (Sutton Publishing Limited, 1997)

David Crane, *Empires of the Dead* (William Collins, 2013)

Lyn MacDonald, *They called it Passchendaele* (Michael Joseph Limited, 1978)

Philip Stevens, *The Great War Explained* (Pen and Sword Military, 2012)

Malcolm Brown, *Tommy Goes to War* (Tempus Publishing Ltd, 2001)

Martin Middlebrook, *The First Day of the Somme 1 July 1916* (Penguin Books Ltd, 1984)

Reginald Turnill and Arthur Reed, *Farnborough; The Story of RAE* (Robert Hale Ltd, 1980)

Michael Renshaw, *Mametz Wood* (Pen and Sword Military, 2014)

Norman Franks, Frank Bailey and Rick Duiven, *Casualties of the German Air Service 1914–1920* (Grub Street, 1999)

Steven John, *Carmarthen Pals* (Pen and Sword Military, 2009)

Gavin Roynon, *Massacre of the Innocents* (Sutton Publishing Limited, 2004)

Olive Murray Chapman, *Across Lapland* (Penguin Books Ltd, 1939)

Reginald Pound, *The Lost Generation of 1914* (Coward-McCann, Inc, 1965)

Philip William Adams, *Idle and Dissolute* (The Memoir Club, 2013)

Peter Hart, *Gallipoli* (Profile Books Ltd, 2013)

Charles H Horton, *Stretcher Bearer!* (Lion Books, 2013)

Gordon Corrigan, *Mud, Blood and Poppycock* (Cassell, 2003)

Rowland Fielding, edited by Jonathan Walker, *War Letters to a Wife* (Spellmount Classics, 2001)

Harold C A Hankins, *A History of The Manchester and Salford Universities Officer's Training Corps 1898–2002* (DP & G Military Publishers, 2002)

Craig Gibson, *Behind the Front: British Soldiers and French Civilians, 1914–1918* (Cambridge University Press, 2014)

Websites

The Long, Long Trail, www.longlongtrail.co.uk
The Aerodrome, www.theaerodrome.com
World War One Photos, www.ww1photos.com
Commonwealth War Graves Commission, www.cwgc.org
The University of Manchester World War 1 Centenary, www.ww1.manchester.ac.uk
Ancestry, www.ancestry.co.uk
The British Newspaper Archive, www.britishnewspaperarchive.co.uk
The National Archives, http://discovery.nationalarchives.gov.uk
The University of Manchester Library Database; ELGAR: Electronic Gateway to Archives at Rylands, http://archives.li.man.ac.uk/ead/

SOURCES OF INFORMATION AND ENDNOTES

The following published and unpublished books, documents, letters, websites have contributed to my understanding of the lives of individual Hulme Hall men.

Common Sources of Information

Commonwealth War Graves Commission website; cwgc.org
National Archives, Kew
[56] Manchester University Roll of Service, published 1922
Hulme Hall Archives, held at the University of Manchester Library, Manchester
Manchester & Salford Universities Officer Training Corps Roll of Honour 1914–1919
1901 and 1911 Census data via Ancestry.co.uk
Marriage records via Ancestry.co.uk

One Hundred Years On

[1] The statement of commendation has been taken from a handwritten note inserted into Henderson's service records, held at the National Archives, Kew, reference WO 339/28623

Acknowledgements

[2] Taken from information regarding Godfrey Hemsley held in the Garton Archive at Lincoln Christ's Hospital School

History of Hulme Hall

[3] Hulme Hall Prospective, held at the University of Manchester Library, Manchester, reference GB HHH/2/10
[4] Dr G N Burkhardt, *Pioneer Hall of Residence in Manchester* (1970). A copy of this document was kindly passed to the Author by Robert Quale.

Calm Before the Storm

[5] Letter written from Harry Pickles to Professor Thomas Tout, dated May October 1912, held at the University of Manchester Library, Manchester, reference GB 133 TFT/1/939/1 11
[6] Warden's report for 1913–14 written by Rev J H Hopkinson, held at the University of Manchester Library, Manchester, reference GB 133 HHH/2/3
[7] Harold C A Hankins, *A History of The Manchester and Salford Universities Officer's Training Corps 1898–2002* (DP & G Military Publishers, 2002)
[8] *The Manchester Evening News* (Wednesday 16 June 1915)

Nothing but Honour

[9] Hulme Hall Chronicle 1916–1920, held at the University of Manchester Library, Manchester, reference GB 133 HHH/2/9/1
[10] Pfeffer is the only German national recorded from all the students who entered Hulme Hall from 1887 until 1919 listed in the Hulme Hall Admission records
[11] Hulme Hall Chronicle 1914–1915, held at the University of Manchester Library, Manchester, reference GB 133 HHH/2/9/1
[12] 10% has been estimated from compiling a list of all Hulme Hall men who served in the Armed Forces at any point between 1914 and 1919
[13] Rowland Fielding, edited by Jonathan Walker, *War Letters to a Wife* (Spellmount Classics, 2001)
[14] Craig Gibson, *Behind the Front: British Soldiers and French Civilians, 1914–1918* (Cambridge University Press, 2014)
[15] Norman Franks and Hal Giblin, *Under the Guns of the German Aces* (Grub Street, 1997)

[16] Hulme Hall Chronicle 1922–1924, held at the University of Manchester Library, Manchester, reference GB 133 HHH/2/9/1

The Great War: 1914-1919

[17] Hulme Hall Chronicle 1916–1920, held at the University of Manchester Library, Manchester, reference GB 133 HHH/2/9/1
[18] Letter written by Robert Harold Bedford to Professor Thomas Tout dated August 1915, held at the University of Manchester Library, Manchester, reference GB TFT/1/88
[19] Letter written by William Wildblood to Professor Thomas Tout dated January 1916, held at the University of Manchester Library, Manchester, reference GB 133 TFT/1/1284
[20] History of 57 Squadron, held at the National Archives, Kew, reference AIR 1/693/21/20/57
[21] 17th Battalion Royal Fusiliers War Diaries, held at the National Archives, Kew, reference WO 95/2643
[22] Rowland Fielding, edited by Jonathan Walker, *War Letters to a Wife* (Spellmount Classics, 2001)

A Supreme and Incorruptible Treasure

[23] Hulme Hall Chronicle 1914–1915, held at the University of Manchester Library, Manchester, reference GB 133 HHH/2/9/1

Ernest Nicholson Cunliffe

Hulme Hall Administration Records 1894–1906, held at the University of Manchester Library, Manchester, reference GB 133 HHH/2/7/2
[24] Hulme Hall Chronicle 1916–1920, held at the University of Manchester Library, Manchester, reference GB 133 HHH/2/9/1
Major E N Cunliffe Service Records, held at the National Archives, Kew, reference WO 374/17245
William Brockbank, *The Honorary Medical Staff of the Manchester Royal*

Infirmary 1830–1948 (Manchester University Press, 1965)
The British Medical Journal, April 26 1919

Arthur Cyril Richards Davies

Hulme Hall Administration Records 1894–1906, held at the University of Manchester Library, Manchester, reference GB 133 HHH/2/7/2
Hulme Hall Chronicle 1914–1915, held at the University of Manchester Library, Manchester, reference GB 133 HHH/2/7/2
Second Lieutenant A C R Davies Service Records, held at the National Archives, Kew, reference WO 374/18166
Lieutenant W Meakin, *History of the 5th North Staffords and the North Midland Territorials (the 46th and 59th Divisions), 1914-1919* (Hughes and Harber Limited, undated)
[25] 5th Battalion North Staffordshire Regiment War Diaries, February 1915 to January 1918, held at the National Archives, Kew, reference WO 95/2685/1

Harold Danby Swift

Hulme Hall Administration Records 1894–1906, held at the University of Manchester Library, Manchester, reference GB 133 HHH/2/7/2
[26] Private H D Swift Service Records, held by the National Archives of Australia, reference B2455 / SWIFT Harold Danby
Red Cross Wounded and Missing record for 7306 Private Harold Danby Swift, published online by the Australian War Memorial

Godfrey Hamilton Hemsley

Hulme Hall Administration Records 1894–1906, held at the University of Manchester Library, Manchester, reference GB 133 HHH/2/7/2
Second Lieutenant G H Hemsley Service Records, held at the National Archives, Kew, reference WO 339/92261
Garton Archive at Lincoln Christ's Hospital School
[27] Courts-martial of the First World War – Staff Sergeant G H Hemsley

Canadian Army Medical Corps: Reference RG150 – Ministry of the Overseas Military Forces of Canada, Series 8, File 649-H-13298, Microfilm Reel Number T-8666

Joseph Percival Maiden

Hulme Hall Administration Records 1907–1915, held at the University of Manchester Library, Manchester, reference GB 133 HHH/2/7/3
Hulme Hall Remembrance Service Sheet, 2001 compiled by Gareth Williams
[28] Joseph Percival Maiden Service Records, ancestry.co.uk – British Army WWI Service Records, 1914-1920
6th Battalion (Inniskilling) Dragoons War Diaries, held at the National Archives, Kew, reference WO 95/1176/3 and WO 95/1160/4

William George Freemantle

Hulme Hall Administration Records 1907–1915, held at the University of Manchester Library, Manchester, reference GB 133 HHH/2/7/3
[29] Extract from a letter written to Rev T Nicklin by William Charles Freemantle in which he wrote extracts from letters received from William's comrades. Letter held in Hulme Hall Administration Records 1907–1915
[30] Extract from newspaper cutting of an obituary of William Freemantle (unknown newspaper and undated), held in Hulme Hall Administration Records 1907–1915
Hulme Hall Chronicle 1916–1920, held at the University of Manchester Library, Manchester, reference GB 133 HHH/2/9/1
West Berkshire War Memorials – http://westberkshirewarmemorials.org.uk/texts/stories/WBP01187S.php
Gerald B Hurst, *With Manchesters in the East* (The Naval & Military Press Ltd, undated)
The Manchester Evening News (Friday 11 June 1915 and Wednesday 16 June 1915)

Harry Thornton Pickles

Hulme Hall Administration Records 1907–1915, held at the University of Manchester Library, Manchester, reference GB 133 HHH/2/7/3
Hulme Hall Chronicle 1916–1920, held at the University of Manchester Library, Manchester, reference GB 133 HHH/2/9/1
9th Battalion West Riding Regiment War Diaries, held at the National Archives, Kew, reference WO 95/2014/1
[31] Letter written by William Wildblood to Professor Thomas Tout, dated May 1915, held at the University of Manchester Library, Manchester, reference GB 133 TFT/1/1284
[32] Obituary written by Professor Thomas Tout, published in *Manchester University Magazine*, 1916, held at John Rylands Library, reference GB 133 UMP/2/3 /12 November 1915–February 1917
Susan Pares, *Displaced by War* (Francis Boutle Publishers, 2015)

William Arthur Wildblood

Hulme Hall Administration Records 1907–1915, held at the University of Manchester Library, Manchester, reference GB 133 HHH/2/7/3
Hulme Hall Chronicle 1916–1920, held at the University of Manchester Library, Manchester, reference GB 133 HHH/2/9/1
Lieutenant W A Wildblood Service Records, held at the National Archives, Kew, reference WO 339/30482
[33] Letter written by William Wildblood to Professor Thomas Tout dated January 1917, held at the University of Manchester Library, Manchester, reference GB 133 TFT/1/1284
[34] Extracts from newspaper cuttings sent to Professor Tout, by William's father, Rev Charles Wildblood, after William's death, held at the University of Manchester Library, Manchester, reference GB 133 TFT/1/1284
Memorial booklet in memory of William Wildblood, held in Professor Thomas Tout collection of letters from William, held at the University of Manchester Library, Manchester, reference GB 133 TFT/1/1284
Yorkshire Rugby Football Union, *Commemoration Book 1914–19 and Official Handbook Season 1919–20* (published by Authority, 1919)
The Wildblood family history website; wildblood.org; maintained by Alan Wildblood

Eyre Spenser Wilkinson

Hulme Hall Administration Records 1907–1915, held at the University of Manchester Library, Manchester, reference GB 133 HHH/2/7/3
Hulme Hall Chronicle 1916–1920, held at the University of Manchester Library, Manchester, reference GB 133 HHH/2/9/1
[35] Letter written by Henry Spenser Wilkinson, father of Eyre, to Professor Thomas Tout dated February 1916, held at the University of Manchester Library, Manchester, reference GB TFT/1/1288
'C' Flight Diary, Volume 1 March 1915–April 1916; No.1 Squadron Royal Flying Corps records, held at the National Archives, Kew, reference AIR 1/1332/204/17/58
1st Battalion City of London (Royal Fusiliers) War Diaries, held at the National Archives, Kew, reference WO/95/1730/0/397
Lieutenant E S Wilkinson Service Records, held at the National Archives, Kew, reference WO 374/74476
Obituary written by unknown author, published in *Manchester University Magazine*, 1916, held at John Rylands Library, reference GB 133 UMP/2/3 /12 November 1915-February 1917

Howard Redmayne Harker

Hulme Hall Administration Records 1907–1915, held at the University of Manchester Library, Manchester, reference GB 133 HHH/2/7/3
Hulme Hall Chronicle 1916–1920, held at the University of Manchester Library, Manchester, reference GB 133 HHH/2/9/1)
Second Lieutenant W R Harker Service Records, held at the National Archives, Kew, reference WO 339/57841
History of 57 Squadron, held at the National Archives, Kew, reference AIR 1/693/21/20/57
57 Squadron Combat Reports March 1917–October 1918, held at the National Archives, Kew, reference AIR 1/1224/204/5/2634
[36] *Supplement to the London Gazette*, 9 January 1918, page 612
Peter Hart, *Bloody April – Slaughter in the Skies over Arras, 1917* (Cassell, 2006)
Jon Guttman, *Reconnaissance and Bomber Aces of World War 1* (Osprey Publishing, 2015)

Norman Franks and Hal Giblin, *Under the Guns of the German Aces* (Grub Street, 1997)
Geoff D Copeman, *Bomber Squadrons at War* (Sutton Publishing Limited, 1997)
Reginald Turnill and Arthur Reed, *Farnborough; The Story of RAE* (Robert Hale Ltd, 1980)

Charles Hamilton Murray Chapman

Hulme Hall Administration Records 1907–1915, held at the University of Manchester Library, Manchester, reference GB 133 HHH/2/7/3
Hulme Hall Chronicle 1916–1920, held at the University of Manchester Library, Manchester, reference GB 133 HHH/2/9/1)
C H M Chapman Service Records, held at the National Archives, Kew, reference ADM 273/6/201
C H Murray Chapman, *Dragons at Home* (Wells Gardner, Darton & Co. Ltd, undated)
Olive Murray Chapman, *Across Lapland* (Penguin Books Ltd, 1939)

Arthur Morton Goodall

Hulme Hall Administration Records 1907–1915, held at the University of Manchester Library, Manchester, reference GB 133 HHH/2/7/3
[37] Hulme Hall Chronicle 1916–1920, held at the University of Manchester Library, Manchester, reference GB 133 HHH/2/9/1

William Orlando Jones

Hulme Hall Remembrance Service Sheet, 2001 compiled by Gareth Williams
Hulme Hall Administration Records 1907–1915, held at the University of Manchester Library, Manchester, reference GB 133 HHH/2/7/3
[38] Hulme Hall Chronicle 1916–1920, held at The University of Manchester Library, Manchester, reference GB 133 HHH/2/9/1
Captain W O Jones Service Records, held at the National Archives, Kew, reference WO 339/23760

The History of the Royal Fusiliers 'UPS' University and Public Schools Brigade (The Times, undated)
The Manchester Evening News, Wednesday 14 November 1917
Ian Connerty, Sir Martin Gilbert, Peter Hart, Lyn MacDonald and Nigel Steel *At the Going Down of the Sun – 365 Soldiers from the Great War* (Lannoo, 2001)

Aubrey Harris

Hulme Hall Administration Records 1907–1915, held at the University of Manchester Library, Manchester, reference GB 133 HHH/2/7/3
[39] Letter written by Aubrey's father to the Rev T Nicklin dated September 1916, held in Hulme Hall Administration Records 1907–1915
Hulme Hall Chronicle 1916–1920, held at the University of Manchester Library, Manchester, reference GB 133 HHH/2/9/1
Lieutenant A Harris Service Records, held at the National Archives, Kew, reference WO 339/18813
21st Battalion Manchester Regiment War Diaries, held at the National Archives, Kew, reference WO 95/1668/1
Michael Stedman, *Manchester Pals* (Leo Cooper, 2004)

Robert Harold Bedford

Hulme Hall Administration Records 1907–1915, held at the University of Manchester Library, Manchester, reference GB 133 HHH/2/7/3
Hulme Hall Chronicle 1916–1920, held at the University of Manchester Library, Manchester, reference GB 133 HHH/2/9/1
[40] Letters written by Robert Harold Bedford to Professor Thomas Tout dated 1915 to 1918, held at the University of Manchester Library, Manchester, reference GB TFT/1/88
[41] Extract of record of Robert being mentioned in despatches from letter written by Robert's father to Professor Thomas Tout dated April 1918, held at the University of Manchester Library, Manchester, reference GB TFT/1/88
Captain R H Bedford Service Records, held at the National Archives, Kew, reference WO 374/5288
6th Battalion Manchester Regiment War Diaries March 1917 to March 1919,

held at the National Archives, Kew, reference WO 95/2660/2

John Hartley, *6th Battalion The Manchester Regiment in the Great War* (Pen & Sword Military, 2010)

Stephen Ambrose Fisher

Hulme Hall Administration Records 1907–1915, held at the University of Manchester Library, Manchester, reference GB 133 HHH/2/7/3

[42] Extract from letter written by Caroline Fisher to Rev T Nicklin, dated 2 October 1916, held within Hulme Hall Administration Records 1907–1915

Hulme Hall Chronicle 1916–1920, held at the University of Manchester Library, Manchester, reference GB 133 HHH/2/9/1

20th Battalion Royal Fusiliers War Diaries, held at the National Archives, Kew, reference WO 95/2423

Terry Norman, *The Hell they Called High Wood* (Pen & Sword Military, 2012)

Harland Watts

Hulme Hall Administration Records 1907–1915, held at the University of Manchester Library, Manchester, reference GB 133 HHH/2/7/3

Hulme Hall Chronicle 1916–1920, held at the University of Manchester Library, Manchester, reference GB 133 HHH/2/9/1

[43] Extract from letter written by Harland Watts to Professor Thomas Tout, dated June 1916, held at the University of Manchester Library, Manchester, reference GB TFT/1/ 1259

7th Battalion South Lancashire Regiment War Diaries, held at the National Archives, Kew, reference WO 95/2081/4

Lieutenant Harland Watts Service Records, held at the National Archives, Kew, reference WO 339/33075

James Grieg Mitchell Henderson

[45] Hulme Hall Administration Records 1907–1915, held at The University of Manchester Library, Manchester, reference GB 133 HHH/2/7/3

Hulme Hall Chronicle 1915–1916, held at the University of Manchester Library, Manchester, reference GB 133 HHH/2/9/1
Second Lieutenant J G M Henderson Service Records, held at the National Archives, Kew, reference WO 339/28623
[44] Captain Reginald Berkley and Brigadier-General William W Seymour, *The History of The Rifle Brigade in the War of 1914–1918 Volume 1 and Volume 2* (N & M Press, 2003)
3rd Battalion Rifle Brigade War Diaries November 1915 to March 1917, held at the National Archives, Kew, reference WO 95/2206/1
4th Battalion Rifle Brigade War Diaries, December 1914 to October 1915, held at the National Archives, Kew, reference WO 95/2262/2
Manchester & Salford Universities Officer Training Corps Roll of Honour 1914–1919

Wilfred Trevelyan

Hulme Hall Administration Records 1907–1915, held at the University of Manchester Library, Manchester, reference GB 133 HHH/2/7/3
Hulme Hall Chronicle 1914–1915, held at the University of Manchester Library, Manchester, reference GB 133 HHH/2/9/1
[46] *The Manchester University Magazine*, Volume XI No.10 June 24th, 1915, held at the University of Manchester Library, reference GB 133 UMP/2/3 /11 October 1914–June 1915
Second Lieutenant W Trevelyan Service Records, held at the National Archives, Kew, reference WO 339/28630
4th Battalion Rifle Brigade War Diaries, December 1914 to October 1915, held at the National Archives, Kew, reference WO 95/2262/2
John Lewis-Stempel, *Six Weeks* (Orion Books Ltd, 2010)

Alfred Edward Holton

Hulme Hall Administration Records 1907–1915, held at the University of Manchester Library, Manchester, reference GB 133 HHH/2/7/3
Lieutenant A E Holton Service Records, held at the National Archives, Kew, reference ADM/196/65

[47] Holton family history on Levantine Heritage website; www.levantineheritage.com/holton.htm
[48] *Supplement to the London Gazette*, 11 January 1919

Alan Higson Smith

Hulme Hall Administration Records 1907–1915, held at the University of Manchester Library, Manchester, reference GB 133 HHH/2/7/3
Hulme Hall Chronicle 1916–1920, held at the University of Manchester Library, Manchester, reference GB 133 HHH/2/9/1
The Sphere, 23rd March 1918
Captain A H Smith Service Records, held at the National Archives, Kew, reference WO 339/15879 and AIR/76/468
[49] *Supplement to the London Gazette*, 25 August 1916

George Hebblethwaite

Hulme Hall Administration Records 1907–1915, held at the University of Manchester Library, Manchester, reference GB 133 HHH/2/7/3
Hulme Hall Chronicle 1916–1920, held at the University of Manchester Library, Manchester, reference GB 133 HHH/2/9/1
Upper Hopton Parish Magazine, August 1916
10th Battalion Lancashire Fusiliers War Diaries, held at the National Archives, Kew, reference WO 95/2012/1
[50] Second Lieutenant G Hebblethwaite Service Records, held at the National Archives, Kew, reference WO 339/46764

James Richard Blue

Hulme Hall Administration Records 1907–1915, held at the University of Manchester Library, Manchester, reference GB 133 HHH/2/7/3
[51] 1901 and 1911 Census Records, ancestry.co.uk
[52] Hulme Hall Chronicle 1916–1920, held at the University of Manchester Library, Manchester, reference GB 133 HHH/2/9/1
Private J R Blue Service Records, held on ancestry.co.uk

1st Battalion Honourable Artillery Company War Diaries, held at the National Archives, Kew, reference WO 95/3118/1
James Pitt, *Battle of Bailescourt Farm February 1917; Cecil's First Battle* (www.newsonfarm.com/BATTLE%20OF%20BAILESCOURT%20FARM%202.doc, June 2007)

William Lawton

Hulme Hall Administration Records 1907–1915, held at the University of Manchester Library, Manchester, reference GB 133 HHH/2/7/3
[53] Extracts from letters received by the Lawton family following William's death, sent to Rev T Nicklin, undated. Extracts held within Hulme Hall Administration Records 1907–1915
Hulme Hall Chronicle 1916–1920, held at the University of Manchester Library, Manchester, reference GB 133 HHH/2/9/1
8th Battalion the South Lancashire Regiment War Diaries, held at the National Archives, Kew, reference WO 95/2081
Second Lieutenant W Lawton Service Records, held at the National Archives, Kew, reference WO 339/36440

William Bigham

Hulme Hall Administration Records 1907–1915, held at the University of Manchester Library, Manchester, reference GB 133 HHH/2/7/3
[54] Newspaper cutting with obituary of William Bigham, held within Hulme Hall Administration Records 1907–1915. Newspaper and date of publication both unknown
Hulme Hall Chronicle 1914–1915, held at the University of Manchester Library, Manchester, reference GB 133 HHH/2/7/24
Second Lieutenant William Bigham Service Records, held at the National Archives, Kew, reference WO 339/2035

Robert George Alexander Dickey

Hulme Hall Administration Records 1907–1915, held at the University of

Manchester Library, Manchester, reference GB 133 HHH/2/7/3

Hulme Hall Chronicle 1916–1920, held at the University of Manchester Library, Manchester, reference GB 133 HHH/2/7/2

Captain R G A Dickey Service Records, held at the National Archives, Kew, reference WO 374/19569

Colne and District Roll of Honour and War Record 1914–1919 (Colne and Nelson Times, 1920)

Steven Howarth, *A Grammar School at War – the story of Ermysted's Grammar School during the Great War* (John Mason, 2007)

Harold James Porter

Hulme Hall Administration Records 1907–1915, held at the University of Manchester Library, Manchester, reference GB 133 HHH/2/7/3

Hulme Hall Chronicle 1914–1915, held at the University of Manchester Library, Manchester, reference GB 133 HHH/2/7/2

[55] Second Lieutenant H J Porter Service Records, held at the National Archives, Kew, reference WO 374/54730

5th Battalion Manchester Regiment War Diaries, held at the National Archives, Kew, reference WO 95/4316

Arthur Lord

Hulme Hall Administration Records 1907–1915, held at the University of Manchester Library, Manchester, reference GB 133 HHH/2/7/3

[57] Hulme Hall Chronicle 1915–1916, held at the University of Manchester Library, Manchester, reference GB 133 HHH/2/7/2

Captain A Lord Service Records, held at the National Archives, Kew, reference WO 339/4008

1st Battalion Welsh Regiment War Diaries January 1915 to October 1915, held at the National Archives, Kew, reference WO 95/2277/4

14th Battalion Welsh Regiment War Diaries January 1915 to October 1915, held at the National Archives, Kew, reference WO 95/2559/3

15th Battalion Welsh Regiment War Diaries January 1915 to October 1915, held at the National Archives, Kew, reference WO 95/2559/4

Genealogy in Hertfordshire website http://www.hertfordshire-genealogy.co.uk/ run and maintained by Chris Reynolds
De Ruvigny's Roll of Honour 1914–24 (Navy & Military Press Ltd)

William Spence

Hulme Hall Administration Records 1907–1915, held at the University of Manchester Library, Manchester, reference GB 133 HHH/2/7/3
[58] Hulme Hall Chronicle 1915–1916, held at the University of Manchester Library, Manchester, reference GB 133 HHH/2/7/2
8th Battalion Royal Fusiliers War Diaries January 1915 to October 1915, held at the National Archives, Kew, reference WO 95/1857/1

Kenneth Barry

Hulme Hall Administration Records 1907–1915, held at the University of Manchester Library, Manchester, reference GB 133 HHH/2/7/3
[59] Letter written by Mrs Barry, Kenneth's mother, dated January 1917, held in Hulme Hall Administration Records 1907–1915
Hulme Hall Chronicle 1916–1920, held at the University of Manchester Library, Manchester, reference GB 133 HHH/2/7/2
23rd Battalion Royal Fusiliers War Diaries January 1915 to October 1915, held at the National Archives, Kew, reference WO 95/1372/3

William Leslie Wood

Hulme Hall Administration Records 1915–1919, held at the University of Manchester Library, Manchester, reference GB 133 HHH/2/7/4
Hulme Hall Chronicle 1916–1920, held at the University of Manchester Library, Manchester, reference GB 133 HHH/2/7/2
Captain W L Wood Service Records, held at the National Archives Kew, reference WO 339/52066
15th Battalion Royal Welsh Fusiliers War Diaries December 1915 to February 1918, held at the National Archives, Kew, reference WO 95/2556/1

[60] *De Ruvigny's Roll of Honour 1914–24* (Navy & Military Press Ltd)

Robert Kennaugh Southward

Hulme Hall Administration Records 1915–1919, held at the University of Manchester Library, Manchester, reference GB 133 HHH/2/7/4
[62] Extract from letter written by Winnie Southward, Robert's sister, dated 17 October 1916, held within Hulme Hall Administration Records 1915–1919
Hulme Hall Chronicle 1916–1920, held at the University of Manchester Library, Manchester, reference GB 133 HHH/2/7/2
[61] 1st Battalion Loyal North Lancashire Regiment War Diaries January 1916 to December 1916, held at the National Archives, Kew, reference WO 95/1270/3

William Frederick Williams

Hulme Hall Administration Records 1915–1919, held at the University of Manchester Library, Manchester, reference GB 133 HHH/2/7/4
Hulme Hall Chronicle 1916–1920, held at the University of Manchester Library, Manchester, reference GB 133 HHH/2/7/2
17th Battalion Royal Fusiliers War Diaries, held at the National Archives, Kew, reference WO 95/2643
Second Lieutenant W F Williams Service Records, held at the National Archives, Kew, reference WO 339/109696

William Barnett Warrington

Hulme Hall Administration Records 1889–1894, held at the University of Manchester Library, Manchester, reference GB 133 HHH/2/7/1
Amanda Taylor, The St James War Memorial Project, *St James Cemetery WW1 Casualties*
Royal College of Physicians – Lives of the Fellows website http://munksroll.rcplondon.ac.uk/Biography/Details/4636
[63] *The British Medical Journal*, William Barnett Warrington Obituary, 15 February 1919

Dudley Collins Francis

Hulme Hall Administration Records 1894–1906, held at the University of Manchester Library, Manchester, reference GB 133 HHH/2/7/2

Second Lieutenant D C Francis Service Records, held at the National Archives Kew, reference WO 374/25465

18th Battalion Royal Fusiliers War Diaries, held at the National Archives, Kew, reference WO 95/2423/2

[64] 5th Battalion York and Lancaster War Diaries, held at the National Archives, Kew, reference WO 95/2805/2

Obituary of Dudley Collins Francis published in the Minutes of the Proceedings of the Institution of Civil Engineers, Volume 204 Issue 1917

Arthur Raymond Marshall

Hulme Hall Administration Records 1906–1915, held at the University of Manchester Library, Manchester, reference GB 133 HHH/2/7/3

[66] Captain A R Marshall Service Records, held at the National Archives Kew, reference WO 339/57175

Captain A R Marshall Royal Garrison Artillery Service Records, held at the National Archives Kew, reference ADM/159/119

[65] Obituary of Arthur Marshall on Marlborough College WWI Centenary Commemoration website, archive.marlboroughcollege.org

Frank Clare Caress

Hulme Hall Administration Records 1906–1915, held at the University of Manchester Library, Manchester, reference GB 133 HHH/2/7/3

Private F C Caress Service Records, via ancestry.co.uk

Lieutenant-Colonel W A V Churton, DSO *1/5th Earl of Chester's Battalion 1914–1919* (The Naval & Military Press Ltd, undated)

Frank Caress Marriage Records via ancestry.co.uk

Thomas Rubie Fawsitt

Hulme Hall Administration Records 1906–1915, held at the University of Manchester Library, Manchester, reference GB 133 HHH/2/7/3
Second Lieutenant T R Fawsitt Services Records, held at the National Archives, Kew, reference WO 339/48301
9th Battalion York and Lancaster War Diaries, held at the National Archives, Kew, reference WO 95/2188
The London Gazette, 20 September 1912
The War Record of Christ's College Boat Club 1914–1918, edited by Simon Martin, Secretary 2008–10
[67] Cambridge House website, http://ch1889.org/

Harry Carrington Farrimond

Hulme Hall Administration Records 1906–1915, held at the University of Manchester Library, Manchester, reference GB 133 HHH/2/7/3
[68] Lieutenant H C Farrimond Service Records, held at the National Archives, Kew, reference WO 339/80697
10th Battalion Royal Fusiliers War Diaries, held at the National Archives, Kew, reference WO 95/2532
The History of the Royal Fusiliers 'UPS' University and Public Schools Brigade (The Times, undated)

Noel Christopher Gornell

Hulme Hall Chronicle 1916–1920, held at the University of Manchester Library, Manchester, reference GB 133 HHH/2/7/2
Second Lieutenant N C Gornell Service Records, held at the National Archives, Kew, reference WO 339/99932
157 Field Company Royal Engineers War Diaries December 1915–March 1919, held at the National Archives, Kew, reference WO 95/1965
http://lancasterwarmemorials.org.uk/memorials/lancaster-g.htm
Lancaster Guardian 13 April, 1918